10/○~/

LORI R. MILLER

31 Days of Mental Health Moments

A month of daily practices to help you cope with the stress and anxiety of your crazy, busy life

MILLER
MENTAL HEALTH SERVICES, LLC

To Joe — the moments with you are the best moments of my day. Thank you for being so patient. :-)

Contents

Preface

Our lives are made up of moments. We know that. But we're so busy and so focused on the future that we forget to focus on the moments we're living in. The decisions and attitudes we allow in our present moments are what determine the choices we make. And those choices ultimately affect our future. So you can see how important a simple moment can be.

What exactly is a Mental Health Moment?

Well, tell me if this describes your workday morning. If you're a commuter who drives, you most likely:

- Drove in the parking lot on two wheels,
- Barely dodged fellow coworkers walking in,
- Lurched into a parking space,
- Piled all of your bags on your shoulders and
- Raced into the building.

Slow down there, turbo. You most likely just defied death at 80 miles an hour on a busy highway, and you may have even taken some calls already. You get to have a few minutes in the car to reset your focus before you go racing in to work. Feeling rushed and frazzled won't help you feel resilient and on top of things.

A *Mental Health Moment* means you choose to take 10 seconds

— or even as long as five minutes — to shift gears and set yourself up for success before you get out of the car. Here are a few basic ideas for a simple mental health moment in your company's parking lot:

Take some deep breaths.

This will get your heart rate and your blood pressure back where it needs to be so you can be the calm one who walks in the door today.

Enjoy putting on your favorite lipstick.

Take a few minutes to carefully apply that beautiful shade you just picked up and then smile at yourself in the mirror.

Watch a funny YouTube video.

Personally, I enjoy anything from comedian Brian Regan. He's hilarious, and laughing will also get that same heart rate and blood pressure down.

Listen to that one song that totally fires you up.

My current one is "Never Give Up" by Sia. It's a great soundtrack to make your grand entrance in to work.

Mental Health Moments can happen anywhere, not just in your car.

It's really more about setting aside five minutes wherever you are to set yourself up for success. Each chapter in this book represents one day in the next 31 days. If you want to start on the first day of the month, that's a great way to keep up with which day you're on. But if you want to get crackin' on making positive change for yourself, you can start today. I'm pretty sure you can handle the math and keep track of the days.

For the next 31 days, find some time to read through each of these daily moments. At the end of each chapter is a section called "In this moment." These are a few suggestions you can do to help you apply what you read. When it comes to learning, application is everything.

Read a chapter in the morning to help set you up for focus and purpose as you go through the day. Or you can read a chapter at night to help you reflect on your day. This will allow you to come up with a good plan for tomorrow.

Don't stress the "when." Find some time in each day to give yourself a *Mental Health Moment!*

Free resources

Go beyond the book

Visit the free companion website to this book at **www.mymen talhealthmoment.com/bookresources.** You'll find a list of additional resources on various topics covered in the book and links to helpful exercises.

Get Mental Health Moments all year

This book is only 31 days long, but you can get *Mental Health Moments* beyond just the one month. Sign up to receive weekly information about how to create your own best mental health moments. I'll also keep you updated on new *Mental Health Moment* books I'm working on and courses to help you apply all that you're learning. Visit **www.mymentalhealthmoment. com/subscribe** to join!

Disclaimer

This book does not provide medical advice and is for informational and educational purposes only. It is not a substitute for professional medical or psychological advice, treatment or diagnosis. If you think you may have an emergency, please dial your local emergency response phone number.

DAY 1: Lessons from the edge of the ocean

"You can't cross the sea merely by standing and staring at the water."
—Rabindranath Tagore

One thing I love about being at the beach is how small it makes me feel. This great big ocean in front of me wasn't made by me. And it certainly isn't being maintained by me. It makes me realize that I really don't have control over anything in my life. I am reminded of that when I'm here.

We are all subject to the laws of nature and other forces that keep things going.

There's a lot of power driving those forces, and there's no way we can impact how the ocean comes in to shore or whether or not the moon decides to come up tonight. That means we have to do the best we can with what we've been given and use what we do have power over.

All of us can make an impact. None of us is too small to be effective and to bring meaning to someone else.

I heard a story about a little boy who went to the beach for the first time. When he got to the shore he saw that the sand was completely covered in starfish. They had been washed up and stranded by the great ocean in front of him.

The little boy was old enough to know that starfish need to be in the water to survive. So, one by one, he began throwing them back into the ocean.

About that time an older man came walking along. He saw this little boy hurling the starfish back into the ocean one at a time. Considering the sheer number of starfish on the shore, this exercise seemed futile to the man.

He strolled up to the little boy and said, "What on earth are you doing?"

The little boy looked up at him, his face furrowed in concern.

"These starfish should be in the water," he said. "I'm trying to help them get back."

The man shook his head.

"Son," he said gravely as he motioned toward the sand. "There's too many to save. And they'll just wash back up anyway."

He put his hand on the boy's shoulder and said, "It doesn't matter."

The little boy looked up at him, his youthful hand cradling a single starfish.

"Sir, it matters to this one."

Do you feel like one tiny person against the giant ocean that life has become today?

Is it easy for you to get overwhelmed with what feels like actual waves of things to do and people to keep happy in your own life? Maybe you feel like the simple things you do go unnoticed, or don't matter. It might seem futile to try, but you don't know what role you may play in someone's life.

What you do matters. And it may matter in a big way to just one.

IN THIS MOMENT

- Look around and listen to what's going on around you right now. Don't be too weird about it where people start wondering what's up with you. :-) But observe your surroundings in this particular moment.
- What are others struggling to do or get done?
- What one thing can you do to help someone get where they need to go today?

DAY 2: What are you running from?

"Avoiding danger is no safer in the long run than outright exposure. The fearful are caught as often as the bold."
— Helen Keller

We find all kinds of ways to avoid discomfort, don't we? We're kind of wired to find ways to run away from pain and uncomfortable feelings. We all fall victim to avoidant behaviors.

When was the last time you ran *toward* a problem? When was the last time you embraced your difficult feelings and just powered through something? If you're like most of us, you find it easier to run from those scary feelings and see if you can avoid confronting your problems head on.

How's that working out for you?

When we struggle with our emotions and face difficult decisions, we can find great comfort in avoiding these experiences altogether.

- Maybe it's easier to put off actually starting on that challenging project if you tell yourself you still need to do more research and planning.

- Maybe it feels better to demolish that pint of ice cream instead of dealing with how you're not handling the strain and stress of work very well.
- Maybe it's easier to stay home on the weekend rather than put yourself out there and possibly get rejected.

We perform these kinds of avoidant behaviors all the time because we think they give us what we need. In fact, they do give us momentary relief from our painful feelings and fears. So in a way, this avoidance works.

But unfortunately it also keeps us from getting to the other side of our pain. And most of our victories are just on the other side of discomfort. If we're not careful, we can look up and realize that we've spent much of our time trying to keep from feeling bad.

"Not feeling bad" isn't the same as moving toward healthy goals. And how long do you think "not feeling bad" will last anyway? So, what's the alternative?

For starters, it's important to accept that we have uncomfortable feelings at times.

We all do. It's okay not to feel okay. And it's okay that you don't want to feel that way. That doesn't mean you're not being a positive person or that you lack leadership skills or that you're emotionally deficient.

It means you're exchanging carbon dioxide for oxygen, like all other humans. You're one of us. Welcome to the show.

Second, stop playing the psychological version of "stop hitting yourself" with your thoughts.

You'll have something like 80,000 thoughts in a day. Do you seriously think you can make a dent in controlling that kind of mental traffic whizzing by? It might be easier to stop fighting, get out of the road and just observe it all going by from the sidewalk. From this vantage point, you can see all the action from a safe distance. You can learn from that, and it doesn't require entertaining every single thing that pops in your head.

Your thoughts are best consumed like fried chicken at a picnic: while the crust is hot and crispy and never after four hours. You do yourself no favors by chewing on old, negative thoughts until they're unrecognizable. Instead:

- Observe and accept your thoughts as part of your experience,
- Take from them what you can, then
- Let them wander on by like your rowdy nephews at that picnic.

Those adorable little darlings are never a problem until you start pointing out how loud they are and try to get them to calm down. So they get even louder. Now all you've done is give them energy and the motivation to keep being loud. Let them run.

If you can do this — if you can start to view your thoughts as less of a judgement about who you are and more as an observable measure of your experiences — you'll find you may need less to escape from and avoid.

Last, you can choose to commit to what you believe in — commit to your values.

Your values aren't the things you feel you should do or that you're expected to do or that everyone else is doing. Instead, it's that deep inner voice that keeps dropping you back to the same exact place. If you know how to look for them, there are some common threads in your life that tell you a lot about who you are and where you want to go. Pay attention to those threads.

This requires some soul searching and a fair amount of imagination. Once you connect with your vision, though, it becomes less important to find ways to run from what's not working. You'll feel the urgency to get started on the things that are important to you.

You can find the courage to run toward your problems and your uncomfortable thoughts.

But that doesn't mean you have to let them stick around. I think that's the part that scares us. If we actually experience our feelings, then they may never go away. Who wants that?

By opening ourselves up to our feelings we actually take away some of their power. Acknowledging those difficult feelings and thoughts lets us find ways to keep them in their place before they take us down the road of rumination and obsessing over everything that's going wrong in our lives.

Running toward your problems won't necessarily solve them, and you may still have days when you feel like a loopy and wide-eyed emoji. But at a minimum you'll be engaging in the very days that make up your life instead of trying to distract yourself.

IN THIS MOMENT

- Think about the last time you avoided a difficult thought or circumstance (e.g., eating that pint of ice cream instead of dealing with your stress at work).
- How did that avoidance help you? How did it hurt you?
- How would your experience be different if you had approached your problem with the intent of letting it be instead of running away?
- What ways could you have practiced accepting your feelings about that issue?
- Write down how you can handle this difficult feeling the next time it comes up.

DAY 3: What's on your mind?

"Your inside creates your outside."
— Richie Norton

When you think about anxiety, what does it look like for you? Is it just in your head?

For many people, anxiety looks like a *panic attack*: an elevated physical response to a stressor that seems to come out of nowhere while you're minding your own business. If you've ever had a panic attack, you know they can be frightening. But there's more to anxiety than "attacks" of anxiety.

Sometimes the signs of anxiety are more subtle. It can be easy to miss those signs or think that because you aren't having panic attacks that you're not dealing with anxiety.

But if you listen closely to some of the things you may be struggling with, you'll see some interesting patterns.

Thinking yourself to death

I call this "playing the tapes." (Read Day 4 for an explanation of this one.) You rehash and review your day over and over again, which serves to effectively keep you out of the present and stuck in the past. When you stack up those challenges against your worries about the future, then you experience anxiety.

Overthinking becomes a desperate way to control a world that is already behind you while trying to second-guess what may happen in the future ahead of you.

Feeling disorganized and forgetful

Do you suddenly find yourself forgetting the simplest things and struggling with basic organizational skills? Or maybe you can't focus on one task long enough to actually complete it. You know this isn't normally what you do. What's happening?

Memory and focus take a big hit when anxiety is in the picture. Because you're overthinking and obsessing over your thoughts, the cognitive abilities you would normally be able to bring to simple tasks are just not available. Your brain has to spend an enormous amount of energy to keep that information handy in your short-term memory so you can grab it when you need it.

If your brain's busy stewing over something that happened at work last month, then there's little room for trying to remember where you put your keys this morning.

Gut feelings

Annoying conditions like heartburn and irritable bowel syndrome are becoming more common, in the workplace especially. These kinds of issues are quite physical, legitimately painful and can make it difficult to focus on your work. While the symptoms are physical, in many cases the root lies in anxiety.

Recent research is showing that your gut is the key to your mood. Your gut produces most of the serotonin your body uses. You may know that serotonin is a key player in boosting mood and controlling depression. The link between the gut and mental health is so strong that many researchers now refer to the gut as the *second brain*.

Have you ever felt butterflies before giving a presentation at work? That's your digestive system absorbing your nervousness and responding with a physical symptom. While we all experience this kind of nervousness at times, chronic anxiety can lead to more long-term, uncomfortable gastrointestinal distress.

Now your body gets into a loop of physical distress and pain, which makes you nervous, which brings on more distress and pain, and so on, and so on.

So if you're struggling with unexplained digestive issues, you may want to ask yourself what else may be going on.

Anger and frustration

Anger is a necessary emotion that tells you when something you want is being blocked from you. All that overthinking and worry about what you're not getting can leave you feeling helpless and powerless. And that's a surefire recipe for anger and frustration.

In my work with children I've noticed that anxiety can be a huge driver in physical aggression and oppositional behaviors. On the surface, those behaviors can look like anger that the child cannot seem to control.

But if you ask questions about recent events in the family or changes in their living situation, you will most likely find transition or major change that has created some instability. The child uses those oppositional behaviors to try to process and express the anxiety they feel about everything changing.

Have you ever felt that way? Do you have change and

transition at work? Is it hard to feel like your home life will ever really settle in? The anger and frustration you feel may be anxiety lurking under the surface.

So what do you do?

To really get mastery over anxiety you have find practical coping skills that work for you. This may mean working with a professional who can help you walk through the specific thoughts and feelings you've been experiencing.

But there are a few things you can do right now that will help you calm yourself and take the edge off.

Are you getting enough sleep?

Sleep deprivation messes with your ability to respond and it shatters your resilience to basic life events. The common wisdom is to get seven to nine hours of sleep a night. That sounds amazing, right?

But if you're only getting four hours that may be really hard for you. That's too much pressure. Why not try to get to bed a half-hour earlier than usual tonight? Put your new bedtime on your calendar and work backwards from there. Don't worry about whether or not you'll actually go to sleep. Just perform the effort of getting to bed on time.

Then, do that again tomorrow. Now you're establishing a ritual your body will come to respect and respond to with its own rhythms. Bodies love rhythms.

Manage anxiety with a deep breathing practice.

Deep breathing is a simple, free and effective way to manage the physiological signs of anxiety. The most effective form of deep breathing is breathing from your diaphragm.

The diaphragm is a muscle that lies right behind your stomach. When the diaphragm expands, it stimulates your *vagus nerve*. Your vagus nerve handles your heart rate, blood pressure, sweat glands — all the processes that make us feel anxious. So stimulating this nerve by deep breathing tells the multiple systems in your body to calm the heck down.

This is a powerful response, and it absolutely works. You can use deep breathing in any situation. Over time, with enough practice, you can recondition your body against that anxiety response just by activating your deep breathing. (Check out **mymentalhealthmoment.com/bookresources** for helpful techniques and apps.)

Get outside and be still

We modern humans spend most of our waking hours indoors. And while we're indoors we spend most of our time with crushing task lists and responsibilities that barely give us time to go to the bathroom, much less reflect on the larger things in life.

Research is showing us what the earth already knew: there are multiple benefits to being outside in nature at least for a few minutes a day. It's as necessary to our bodies as staying hydrated. You don't need your own wildlife preserve, and you don't have to live near the beach. Place yourself outdoors and put your feet in the grass, or pick a random wildflower or flowering weed. Take a few minutes to remind yourself that you're not designed to just "get things done."

Check out Day 23 for a few more reasons to bring more nature into your life.

The most important thing to know is that you do have control over your anxiety.

I know it doesn't feel that way when you experience it. But with some dedication and commitment to simple and effective practices, you can get some mastery over your everyday anxiety.

IN THIS MOMENT

- Do you recognize any of these symptoms of anxiety in yourself?
- What are some other ways your anxiety shows itself in your daily life?
- Pick one of the three areas to start developing a practice (sleep, be still, deep breathing) and schedule time for it in your days for **this week only**.
- At the end of the week, write down a few areas where you noticed a positive difference.
- Celebrate it, then do it again next week!

DAY 4: Stop playing the tapes

"You'll never plough a field by turning it over in your mind."
— *Irish Proverb*

Have you ever replayed the awkward moments and uncomfortable interactions of the day in your head? We all make those weird comments or wish we had responded in a better way to something.

But do you constantly have that on rewind? Do you play it back over and over in your mind until you exhaust yourself?

I call that "playing the tapes."

It's fine to replay the day to make sure you didn't miss anything. But it's another thing entirely to keep focusing on what you got wrong. Instead of reflecting and learning, you use the tapes to beat yourself up.

One interesting thing I hear from a lot of my clients is how hard it is to stop overthinking everything so much. Overthinking is a casualty of our modern life. There's always so much coming at us on a daily basis that requires critical thinking and decisions. And there's so much information out there that tells us how to process everything that's happened to us and how to improve ourselves. That's fine.

But when this self-examination crosses over into self-doubt and paralysis because of all the mistakes you've made, then overthinking is a problem. So much of what stresses us out, especially at work, is how we are thinking about our stress.

- Does a challenging interaction with your boss wear you out?
- Or is the film review you play back in your head the part that wears you out?

We play the tapes to try to read into things that people say or do. And we spend valuable energy trying to assess our role in all of it when we may not have a role at all.

How do you stop playing the tapes in your head?

Play back things from your day that actually went well.

I mean, why wouldn't this be your first strategy? My guess is you do more things right in a day than you do wrong. Those good things are the low-hanging fruit, and that's always the best stuff. Start picking the good stuff.

Change the wording you use when you look back on your day.

Have compassion for yourself. What things could you do better next time? Where were the learning opportunities today? Every day has learning opportunities. Always focus on the learnings.

Relax your standards. Maybe you said something you wish you hadn't. That's okay. There's no way you are going to communicate 100% of the things perfectly 100% of the time. I've seen some of the most polished professional speakers say the dumbest things. That's just how it goes sometimes. And those same professional speakers will tell you that you have to have a short memory in those moments.

Stop the tape here and move on.

Put yourself in others' shoes.

Think about the last time someone said something really awful, maybe at work. My guess is that you can't easily remember a specific incident. In the same way you're struggling to come up with something specific, others are reviewing your awful moments in the same way. Very few people linger on your shortcomings. They really do move on quickly because they're focused on their own perceived shortcomings.

Maybe you didn't handle things today exactly the way you wanted to, but other people weren't analyzing you nearly as much as you're analyzing yourself right now.

The tapes we play back in our heads are not documentaries based on facts. They're dramas that we've edited to fit our perception of our world. Challenge yourself to stop playing the tapes and focus on what's ahead of you.

IN THIS MOMENT

- Look back over your day or your week. Find ways to encourage yourself for what you got right. It can be a small thing; everything matters. You might be surprised what you uncover.
- If you simply must play the tapes, review them to see where you can improve. What can you try next time that might help you get where you want to go? Make it about your results.
- Visualize yourself hitting the "stop" button. Picture yourself grabbing your notes and leaving this dark film room to re-enter your life in the light.

DAY 5: Worry less and learn to let go

*"Worrying is carrying tomorrow's load with today's strength —
carrying two days at once. It is moving into tomorrow ahead of
time. Worrying doesn't empty tomorrow of its sorrow,
it empties today of its strength."*
— Corrie ten Boom

Worry creates a mess inside your head. You can take a perfectly nice day — with vibrant sunshine, birds singing their first songs of the day, the beautiful glisten of morning dew on the grass — and you can mess all of that up with your worries. Give yourself five minutes to start thinking about what's not working in your life and:

- Those birds will sound warbled and annoying,
- The sun will get too hot, and
- The dew will have now attracted mosquitos who can't seem to stop feasting on you.

How did you get here so fast? We know worry isn't helpful. We don't need to learn that. But how do you let go of worry each day? How does that work in real life? How do you face the day knowing there are a million possible scenarios out there that

19

could take you down any road?

Worry is a decision you make.

If worry is a real problem for you, then it's probably the first decision you're making each day.

- Before you get out of bed, you're already wondering what your boss is going to throw on you today.
- If you don't leave home on time you worry you'll get caught up in the crazy traffic.
- Your kid's teacher will probably call you *again* today because Johnny just won't sit still in class.
- You're already feeling overwhelmed, and you're worried that you won't get it all done.

None of these worries are things you control. But making the decision to give those things space in your head before you brush your teeth? That's all you. And what follows this first decision to worry is the feeling of dread about the day. Not about any one thing in particular. Just an overall sense of dread that you can't shake.

Does that feel real to you? You can change this, but you have to make a deliberate effort to believe you can change it.

You have to be the one to make the change.

No one can take this one for you. If it's Monday, maybe you heard in church over the weekend about how God doesn't want you to worry, that you can give your worry and anxiety to Him. Or maybe you read a great book from one of your favorite influencers about how your thinking shapes everything. Change your thinking, change your life.

Sounds easy enough, right? You can interpret either of those as some magic formula, where one grand effort gets you where you want to go. If you give God your worries on Sunday, then Monday will magically be worry-free. Or you close that influencer's book and feel pretty amped up about seeing all that great success from changing your thinking.

But by the next day, you're right back to hot sun and mosquitoes. Both God and that influencer would tell you that you need to do daily work to free yourself from that worry habit. You won't nail it on day one or maybe even day 12. In fact, you may very well still be worrying on day 12. It takes time to change a habit.

Worry is a habit to change, not a condition to improve.

And like any other habit, you have to decide you will change it and come up with a plan for what that looks like. The answer is simple but not easy.

Here's one way to deal with worry and find ways to let go of some stuff. Start your day with a *Worry-Less Action Plan*. Fancy name, right? Here are the basic principles.

List exactly what you're worried about today.

Be detailed. Give yourself something visible to look at.

One of the hardest things about worry is how it creates confusion and chaos and sends random thoughts bouncing off the inside of your head. After a while you're not really sure what you're worried about. You just know you're worried. It's all jumbled together in one big, giant worrisome hairball.

Give that worry some space and a voice so you can actually see it.

What do you own?

Look at your list. Where are the areas where you feel responsible? Do you feel like you could be doing more in some area that you're not engaged in right now? Can doing that action take away some of that worry?

Or are you taking on responsibility that doesn't belong to you? This is important to figure out. Many of the things we worry about we may not even have a role in. It sucks to worry about things we can't actually do anything about.

Write down a few statements about who you are.

What do you bring to this situation? This takes your focus off of what's not happening and puts it on how you can influence what's actually going on.

Are you a good problem solver? Use your capacity to find solutions to generate some possibilities. Start applying your problem-solving skills to those things.

Are you reliable and steady? Write down specific statements to remind yourself that even though you're not sure how things will turn out, your ability to show up matters. Write down a few ways how your showing up could change the situation.

Think of as many things as you can about who you are. This is the best way to defeat worry. You are countering those worrisome thoughts — which may or may not be true —with what you know to be true about you. So letting go of worry feels a little less like a faith leap into the unknown, and more like a lever you can pull that's right in front of you.

Do this every day.

Write down what you're worried about, which of those worries you can actually do something about, and document how you can influence your situation.

That's it. That's the *Worry-Less Action Plan.*

If you're really jazzed about doing this, you can download this exercise in a printable format at **mymentalhealthmoment.com/bookresources**.

This isn't a plan to address the actual things you're worried about.

Get in the daily habit of addressing your thoughts about your worry and your ability to handle it.

Do this when you first wake up. You don't have to get up at 5 a.m. But it may mean you get up 15 minutes earlier.

Do this before you turn on any other input for the day. In fact, I would suggest while you're working through creating this new habit, maybe you don't watch that morning news show or catch up on the news on your phone while drinking your coffee. There are a million things the news people will tell you to worry about. Almost none of those things involve you.

Try this for a week and chart your level of worry today and every day for the next week. **Download the *Worry-Less Action Plan*** to get a worry scale to help you track your progress over the next week.

Every fiber in your being will tell you this is stupid.

"This won't work. Worry is worry, and that's how it goes." Is that what your most helpful brain is saying right now?

Well, what would you say to a random stranger who walked up to you and told you, completely unsolicited, something you knew wasn't true? You would either ignore them because you think they might be crazy or refute their statement with what you knew to be true.

You can do the same here. Don't take your unsolicited thoughts at face value. You get to choose who you will be this day and what you'll believe about yourself and your world. No matter what happens to you today, this one is all you.

IN THIS MOMENT

- Visit **mymentalhealthmoment.com/bookresources** and download the *Worry-Less Action Plan*.
- Don't worry about making a big splash here. We're not generating any grand epiphanies about how to focus on the future.
- Today focus on creating this one new, Worry-Less habit.
- Write down or say out loud that you trust yourself and believe that who you are can make a difference in how your life turns out.

DAY 6: Serve your neighbor, serve yourself

"If you could only sense how important you are to the lives of those you meet; how important you can be to the people you may never even dream of. There is something of yourself that you leave at every meeting with another person."
— Fred Rogers

When you're in the thick of your life, it's kind of hard to see the impact you're making. If you're a stay-at-home parent, you don't always connect the one million dots in each day with some greater purpose. At work, life can take you down some pretty jagged paths, and it's hard to see exactly how your good work is really moving any bars at all.

It's easy to think it's all just not leading anywhere. Maybe you feel like you're in the world's biggest roundabout, and you keep seeing the same signs over and over again. How can you change the world if you keep going in circles and doing the same things? Maybe you don't need to change the world, necessarily, but you feel like you're spinning your wheels for very little benefit.

Serve others with simple actions.

Recently I watched a documentary about Fred Rogers called *Won't You Be My Neighbor?* If you're old enough, you'll remember Fred Rogers as Mister Rogers. For more than three decades he hosted a children's show called *Mister Rogers' Neighborhood.* The show featured Mister Rogers and his friends — humans and puppets alike — as they lived and supported each other as part of a close-knit community. The show was in its prime during a time of constant cultural change in the world. Fred used his show as a platform to help kids walk through some difficult concepts, like war, racial segregation, divorce and even death.

What struck me about the documentary film was that it wasn't a typical documentary about his early life and his motivation for creating the show. It focused mostly on his impact: to his audience, to his show crew and ultimately, to the nation. Mister Rogers wasn't flashy or larger than life; he was a kind neighbor who liked to wear sweaters. He modeled what it can look like to be engaged in the lives of others around you. Mister Rogers was a servant of others. And his message was kind, simple and clear.

He demonstrated these concepts over an astounding 895 episodes through stories, music and illustrations. I'm sure at times he felt like he'd been on that same roundabout with you. Telling the same stories, repeating the same messages. Did it really help? Should he be more like everyone else? Should he still be doing this at all?

I'm sure it was tempting to think beyond that small neighborhood or expand into something more attention-getting. But the basic format of the show didn't change too much. Fred didn't try to compete with the more complex animation that eventually came on the scene in children's entertainment. He didn't resort to the game of capturing eyeballs for eyeballs' sake. His impact came from his steady pursuit of his principles and convictions in the same way, day after day after day. What can we learn from Mister Rogers?

You don't need to be someone else to be effective.

Fred's show started at a time when other TV shows were using clowns and comedy gags to spread their message. Mister Rogers was never anyone other than Fred. He didn't create a persona that others thought would be more interesting or that would appeal to his audience's insecurities. He was authentic and purely himself. How else do you explain a guy in a sweater and sneakers talking about love and kindness becoming a national icon?

Sweat the right small stuff.

Mister Rogers also taught us that you can show others what a life of healthy pursuits and meaningful purpose looks like with everything you do, even the small stuff. Much of his show centered around the tiniest tasks like feeding the fish, taking care of plants, and talking to neighbors. He knew the children in his audience were watching him consider life's larger issues while at the same time taking care of everyday responsibilities.

He showed them that even though there are challenges in our world, the basics of life do go on. We're so focused on having a powerful impact on the world. But it's just as much our responsibility to change our neighborhood and take care of

27

our own homes even if no one sees it. He showed us what that looks like 895 times.

Complexity doesn't mean better.

The most powerful things in life are usually the simplest ones. Mister Rogers had a clear, concise message that never wavered over all those years: *You are worthy of being loved and capable of showing love to others.* He knew exactly what he wanted his audience to know, and he used that as his GPS for 33 years. Anything more than that would have muddied the waters.

I think that's an important distinction because we find so many ways to complicate our lives, don't we? We always think more education is the key or taking on more responsibility or crafting some image that we think others want to see. In the end, our simple, consistent approach is usually what gets us through.

You will never have all the answers.

This was the biggest takeaway from the documentary film for me. Even when you have great impact — and who had more impact than Mister Rogers? — you still aren't going to have all the answers.

Fred's last show aired just a couple of weeks before the tragic events of September 11, 2001. In the days that followed he was asked to record a public service announcement to speak to parents about the importance of talking to their kids and showing them safety and trust. A member of his crew talked about how overwhelmed Fred was during that shoot. He wondered what he could possibly say that would help in the wake of such an evil event. Despite all the years of guiding kids through some pretty scary and tragic days, even Mister Rogers didn't have the answer for *this* one.

You aren't always going to get the answers, and the dots may not seem to ever really connect despite all that you accomplish. That is one of the bigger mysteries in life, and it's not easy to accept. But even in those moments where you feel like you're spinning, you can find impact by staying in that roundabout a bit longer, taking care of those who need you and modeling kindness where you can. Serving others in a healthy way with what only *you* can bring is the best stress reliever anywhere.

IN THIS MOMENT

- Look back over the past few days. Where do your responsibilities lead you? Who succeeds because you show up consistently every day?
- What could you do more of that would have a greater impact on others?
- What can you let go of that's not contributing in a healthy way to your "neighborhood?"

DAY 7: Keep your emotions in check

"Incredible change happens in your life when you decide to take control of what you do have power over instead of craving control over what you don't."
—Steve Maraboli

Regulating your emotions can be hard sometimes. Things can come at you suddenly and you find yourself grappling with strong emotions. How do you prepare yourself to keep your emotions in check so you can use them in a healthy way?

Well, there's no one way to do it. But there are a few intentional things you can do to ensure you use your healthiest emotions to stay resilient to what comes your way. You can learn to regulate your emotions in a few simple ways and help manage your stress.

Understand what keeps you functioning every day.

What are the main drivers for you in your day? These are the things that will make your day seem a lot harder if they're missing. For me, I have three things that are non-negotiable to help me function well in a day. These are the things that I absolutely make sure that I get done every day.

The first one is sleep.

Everything hinges on me getting good sleep. It feels like a different day when I'm sleep-deprived. I have a hard time managing my emotions on these days. Steer clear of me. You've been warned.

The next one is downtime.

I'm pretty introverted. Even though I love engaging with people, I know that in order to keep engaging with people I need to spend time alone. Being alone recharges my batteries. I try to get at least an hour every day. That's the amount of time that works for me.

The third one is food.

I can't even think straight when I'm hungry. And I've noticed that I feel especially exasperated if I'm trying to handle something challenging, and I'm hungry. So I always have healthy snacks around.

Exercise is super important, too.

This one comes in at a close fourth place for me. Exercise helps me relax my tight shoulder muscles, which is where all my stress lives. I get this really nice, relaxed feeling all over after taking a walk.

Honestly, though, if I miss exercise one day I can still function pretty well. So if something has to go, it's usually exercise. If I go without one of these other three above, it's noticeable to me

31

and others around me.

Identify two or three things in your day that you know help you function well. Then prioritize those things in your day and make them happen before anything else.

Use mindfulness to help regulate your tough feelings.

Mindfulness is one of those hard-to-define words that gets easily misunderstood. Mindfulness is basically staying in the moment and using all of your senses to experience that one moment. Engaging in mindful activities takes you out of your planning, analyzing and goal-setting mode and puts you in a place where you can experience that moment for what it is — good or bad — with no expectations.

Meditation is a form of mindfulness. But you don't have to stick with meditation to be mindful. One of my favorite mindful activities is washing dishes by hand. There's something about feeling the warm, soapy water on my hands and seeing dishes get clean. For you that may be feeling the texture of soft dirt in your hand while gardening. Or sitting in a pretty setting with beautiful, fragrant flowers. It can be enjoying the sound and feel of a paintbrush moving across a canvas. The sky's the limit on this one.

Mindfulness is powerful when it uses all of your senses to bring you into the present. This is important in helping to regulate your emotions because it gives you a break from all of that constant planning and anxiety about the future. Find a few things in your life that allow your senses to experience what's happening around you right now and take you out of your head.

Practice acceptance.

We spend so much time trying to keep our emotions from overwhelming us. But sometimes they just do. So go with it. Even though it's scary, you will survive it, I promise. Let the emotion wash over you like a wave. But do this in a nonjudgmental way. Instead of berating yourself for feeling so emotional, take a deep breath and allow yourself to simply be an observer of how the emotion feels in your body.

- Do you feel it in your chest?
- Does it stay there or does it move to another part of your body?

Instead of fighting it, you can observe and follow what that emotion is doing and where it's going. You'll find it's easier to accept that it's happening and ride it out. Then you get to let it go.

IN THIS MOMENT

- Find your own main drivers for your day. What are the things that make a difference when you miss them? Make them happen as much as you can.
- Start finding opportunities to experience the present through mindfulness. Let go of the chase for productivity and results for a few minutes today and notice what's happening around you.
- Practice accepting that you have these powerful emotions.
- Remind yourself that you can handle how you feel.

DAY 8: Focus on the nuts in front of you

"Let your eyes look directly forward, and your gaze be straight before you."
— Proverbs 4:25

Have you ever been so wrapped up in something fun or different that you kind of forgot for a minute that you were stressed or upset? That's kind of the goal of mindfulness. I know we think of mindfulness as meditation or yoga or other activities that we can channel our minds into. But mindfulness is even easier than that. It's really more about finding ways to access the present moment, however you do it.

Recently I was chopping nuts by hand for a homemade granola recipe. I know, I could've used a food processor, but I was trying to be quiet in the kitchen. I had put all of the different nuts on the cutting board at the same time — almonds, cashews, walnuts, pecans. These nuts all have different textures and respond in different ways to chopping motions. Once I really got going, I realized I was making lots of different shapes depending on how I turned the knife.

Since the almonds are harder, some of them scooted across the room when the knife hit them. The walnuts stayed right where they were and made distinct shapes. The softer cashews folded without a fight. I realized after about 10 minutes that I'd been chopping for a good little while. In fact, I might have reached the point of mincing them.

The only things that existed in that moment were me and a pile of nuts.

I was so focused on what I was doing in that moment and seeing all the colors and shapes take place that I kind of lost track of time. This is why it takes me forever to cook, which is why I don't do so much of it anymore. But it illustrates mindfulness really well, I think.

I honestly wasn't thinking about what I was going to do with all those nuts once they were chopped, and I really wasn't thinking about where they had come from or how much they cost. And I definitely wasn't so meditative that I was emptying my mind or focused on my breathing. I wasn't trying to make this a "thing." I was completely engaged in that activity, creating my little stash of nuts there on the kitchen counter. Maybe I missed my calling as a squirrel. I would've missed all that if I would've just thrown them all into the food processor and whacked them in less than 10 seconds.

You can make mindfulness a thing.

Research is now showing that this kind of mindfulness is a critical part of handling stress. A recent study from the University of Washington showed that teenage girls who reported stress-induced headaches showed a reduced number of those headaches — 40 percent in fact — after practicing mindful art therapy techniques. The art therapy included working with oil paints, trying different mediums and immersing themselves in that experience for 50 minutes. And they found this result in just two sessions a week.

What's interesting is that the teens didn't report that their overall stress levels had improved, merely that their headaches had been reduced. But riddle me this: If you've ever had a stress-induced headache, then doesn't it impact your performance and how well you feel on any given day? Any kind of relief like this can reduce your stress if it reduces your pain.

As a side note, teens report higher levels of stress than adults, most of it related to school. That's a recipe for work-related stress for this cohort in a few years. It's worth all of us getting some understanding about finding mindful ways to handle stress.

Immerse yourself in present moments.

Our modern life is turning up the dial all the time, and we have to be the ones to slow it down. You are the one who can ground yourself for at least a few minutes and notice where you are. Being engaged in your current moment gives you the best shot to walk through your difficult emotions with purpose and understanding.

Here's what's cool. If you can't sit still long enough to meditate or develop a breathing practice, then this kind of mindfulness is for you. Because you don't have to sit still. You just have to pay attention to one thing right in front of you for a wee bit of time.

You should probably pick something more interesting than chopping nuts to bring you back to your present moment. It can be anything that can engage all your senses. Find something that captures your attention but doesn't require anything of you.

IN THIS MOMENT

· When you feel the weight of your responsibilities today, take a minute to notice where you are. What can you slow down and just observe?
· What's around you that you can experience without needing it to turn out a certain way?
· Find those opportunities all around you.

DAY 9: Find your own carefree

"What a lot of us do is that we stay so busy, and so out in front of our life, that the truth of how we're feeling and what we really need can't catch up with us."
— *Brené Brown*

My son got married this year. It's hard to believe that the little toddler who used to stand in his diaper next to the living room window and wave at the guys on the back of the trash truck... is now a married man. That was so fast.

I wanted to drink in all the fun and happiness in the weeks before the wedding. I wanted to experience every emotion and feeling. My son and his wife looked at each other as if they could see their future together in the way they smile. Literally nothing else mattered in that moment. Sitting there watching all this, I wasn't thinking about how I was going to get through all my emails, or how much paperwork I had to do, or if there was going to be time to fit in all my writing sessions for this week.

That day in my life, those moments watching them start their new life, was simply...carefree. It wasn't so much that I didn't have a care in the world. It was more about what I chose to focus on in that moment. All that other stuff didn't make the cut that day. Not even close. I liked feeling carefree very much.

What does it mean to be carefree?

When I think of carefree, I think of running through a field of tulips or maybe letting your hair run wild and free in the wind. It's silly, but that's my visual. If you're a taskmaster like me, being carefree sounds slightly horrifying. It means something else is probably not getting done while you're running through all those tulips.

It took me a while to even put that word on what I was feeling that day at the wedding. Carefree, really? I guess I equate being carefree with fun. They're really not the same thing, are they? Fun sounds like a specific event, like Disney World or a trip to New York City. Being carefree is less about an event. It's more about letting go of what's pulling on me.

Do you ever feel like this? Like everything's pulling on you all at the same time? Wouldn't it be nice to not feel that pressure for a nanosecond? You can actually make that happen for yourself.

What do you care about?

Feeling carefree is less about not having any cares at all but caring more about what's important to you. There's no magic formula or mantra for being carefree. When I decide to focus and give my attention to one thing that matters to me, everything else seems to kind of fall away on its own. I feel room and space around me to breathe a bit. So carefree is a place I can choose to go anytime I want.

There are some terrific benefits of choosing to live in a

carefree state of mind that help you with stress.

Choosing to be carefree takes you out of that "just existing" mode.

I know you know what I'm talking about. It's not hard to fill your life up with so much stuff to do that you feel like you're just checking the boxes. And you get to do it all again tomorrow. Same time, same station, same snacks.

Choosing to be more carefree means maybe you leave a few boxes unchecked today. Stop the hamster wheel for a minute and experience one different thing, something that's not on your list. Sometimes this is enough to help you feel like you can breathe again.

Being carefree is a slam dunk when it comes to staying in the present moment.

You can't be carefree and be thinking about next Tuesday's meeting, or stewing over how your mechanic ripped you off last week. Most of our stress and anxiety is wrapped up in the moments we're not currently living in. I mean, your life is happening right now, isn't it? Choosing to give yourself a carefree moment gives you a shot at actually experiencing that.

Finding carefree moments helps you let go of your stress.

You've probably had that experience on vacation when you finally let go of your to-do list and then you're like, "What was I thinking? Why do I let that stuff bother me? I'm totally gonna stop doing that!"

You get clarity in that moment because it's so obvious that letting go is giving you energy and strength. But honestly, you can have that realization on a smaller level every day. When you stop and make the choice to experience where you are in any given moment, you take your stress down a notch.

Carefree moments means stopping the crazy busy.

We've allowed ourselves to become slaves and martyrs to our schedules and the expectations of others. We make time for things and people we know probably don't add much value. In doing so, we use up our most valuable commodity: our time.

Trying to do it all and satisfy your to-do list may temporarily soothe that knot in your gut. But later, I'm guessing when you're trying to sleep, that same gut might also be whispering to you, "This isn't really cutting it, is it? How do I get off this crazy, busy wheel? When does my good life start?"

You have to define this one for yourself.

What's carefree for me may seem ridiculous to you so I can't give you a recipe here. The truth is that most of us are trying to do too much. And much of what we do on any given day is not that important, if we're honest.

Life isn't just about getting stuff done and achieving goals. There's a rich tapestry of experiences that we're missing out on because we're bound up by our task-centered existence. Choose to find a few random, carefree moments in your days and see if it doesn't change your outlook on your stress.

IN THIS MOMENT

- Learn to qualify the things and people that occupy your time.
- Ask yourself what you're choosing to hang on to in your life today that's keeping you busy and blocking you from that carefree life you see in your head.
- Today, find one thing you can give up to free yourself up.

DAY 10: Connect your self

"Don't so focus on what you love to do that you neglect what needs to be done."
— Max Lucado

Self-care is definitely one of the most important things you can do to feel healthy and strong, physically and mentally. But when I say self-care, what images come up in your mind?

- Maybe you see a lady with cucumbers on her eyes getting a facial while holding a mimosa.
- Or maybe you see someone sitting criss-cross applesauce on a yoga mat at the beach.
- Your mind's eye may see a group of women out having Sunday brunch and laughing together.

Self-care is indeed all of those things. But it's not limited to the things that you set aside special time for. The whole point of self-care is to replenish and recharge. That means self-care has to happen on a regular basis.

So while a spa day or a Sunday brunch with your besties is a terrific way to let your hair down and connect, that kind of self-care can get expensive. And I'm guessing it's pretty hard for everybody to schedule, too.

Here's the thing to know.

Self-care isn't about indulging yourself.

Self-care is about giving back to yourself and filling your own cup. Every day. I'm guessing you're pouring from that cup a lot every day.

As a therapist I have to be intentional about self-care to make sure I have what I need to help others. So for me that means things like exercise, good sleep, and eating healthy food. Those three practices are gold-standard ways to care for yourself every day.

If you have a stressful job with a lot of responsibility or you're a caregiver for an aging parent, you absolutely should be doing these three things every day. That's you caring for yourself in the same way that you're caring for others.

Self-care can take on some other forms, though. Reading is my self-care. This has been the case since I was old enough to pick up a book or newspaper. Reading gives me knowledge, increases my vocabulary, and helps me find meaning and insight in my own experiences. When I feel like I need to recharge, reading is the first place I go. It allows me to give back to myself and invest in what I might need tomorrow to show up for others.

When I'm reading, though, I'm not taking care of some other important things that are on my list. This isn't selfish. Taking time to read is an act of empathy and compassion towards me. It's my way of saying to myself, "I care about you, and I want you to be well."

As a society we really suck at basic self-care.

We go from thing, to thing, to thing with no break in between. Unfortunately we have taught this to our youngest generations. Already, Generations Y, Z, and whoever is coming after that are already struggling with anxiety from being overscheduled and worried about the future.

We keep pushing so hard until we kind of melt down. Then we feel like we need a large block of time to recuperate from everything. So we schedule a spa day, and we enjoy it. But how do you keep from getting to the point where you feel like you have to set aside an entire day to recover from your life?

You need a better strategy, a plan to make sure you have what you need every day to stay resilient to all the random stuff that happens to you. How do you find time for self-care in your busy day?

You can schedule self-care in your calendar like anything else.

I know that sounds kind of like a duh, but it can be challenging to pull off because it may not feel as important as your son's soccer practice. But when you see that entry on the calendar, then you're forced to do something with it. If the soccer practice runs late, fine. Move your self-care time to a different slot. Scheduling it at least puts self-care on your radar.

Do yourself a favor and create a recurring entry on your calendar for whatever will help you hit the pause button in your relentless push to get stuff done. Try making it the first thing you put in your schedule when you do your planning.

Find more time for self-care by simply tagging it on to something else.

I used to work really close to the beach. Many days I commuted home on the two-lane road that ran next to the beach instead of taking the busy four-lane highway. This made it easy to drop in and get some "beach therapy" on my way home. It wasn't an extra trip because I had to go by there to get home anyway. And I didn't bring a whole bunch of beach paraphernalia with me so I couldn't make the trip a "thing."

I just got out of the car and sat in the sand, business-casual wardrobe and all. That time became a buffer to help me purge some of the day's stress before I went home. My family learned to appreciate it, too, because it meant I brought a little less stress home with me.

What are some things you can do to recharge your battery in the middle of other tasks you're already doing? Can you enjoy a quick browse through your favorite bookstore while you're waiting for your son's soccer practice to be over (do we even still have bookstores?) Maybe you can you sit in your car and enjoy your favorite smoothie for a few minutes while you're out running errands.

You're the master here. Get creative and find ways to inject self-care in your day in small ways. If you feel like life is running you over and you're having trouble dealing with everyday stuff, getting a handle on your self-care is a good place to start.

When life gets real, good self-care is sometimes the first thing to go because it feels like a luxury. But it may be the deciding factor in helping you feel less overwhelmed about your life. Find ways to care for yourself every day and see if you don't feel more empowered to make better decisions in your life.

IN THIS MOMENT

- Make a short list of things you love to do but rarely make time for. This is a good way to know what might recharge your spirit in big ways.
- List a few pockets of time today where you can steal away for a few moments by yourself. That self-care time is there for you if you look for it now. You'll lose it later once the day gets rolling.
- Spend a few minutes right now practicing your deep breathing discipline. This is self-care at its finest because it affects so many physical and mental processes.

DAY 11: What spoons can teach you about stress

Appearances to the mind are of four kinds. Things either are what they appear to be; or they neither are, nor appear to; or they are, and do not appear to be; or they are not, and yet appear to be. Rightly to aim in all these cases is the wise man's task."
— *Epictetus*

Life in the 21st century feels pretty extra. I think we all know instinctively that we're trying to take in too much and do too much. It's the scourge of our modern life. Even on the days where things do come together well, we still leave some things on the table.

And that can create anxiety if we don't frame it well.

When I think about my previous corporate life, one stressor stands out above all the others – the relentless, daily focus on output. My task then was to get big stuff completed and out the door every single day. (My actual job description involved words like *synergies*, *cross-functional* and *liaison* but output was basically the job.) My inbox was full of emails every day from my boss about the status of the project du jour. When could she expect to see the completed product, and really, how much longer would it take? My day wasn't successful unless I had delivered all of the things on my list.

Since then I've realized that in those days I was trading the best of my energy and focus every day for small returns. I would start each day feeling as if I had limitless energy and focus. But by lunchtime, I was wondering through a splitting headache how I could already be so far behind. At the end of the day, after scrambling all afternoon, I was exhausted emotionally and physically. I felt like I had very little to show for all this effort I had just put out.

Apparently I didn't understand how to allocate and spend my daily spoons. Allow me to explain.

The Spoon Theory

The spoon theory was first shared by Christine Miserandino in describing to a friend what it's like to live with a chronic illness. In her case, the illness was lupus. She wanted her friend to understand what it's really like to perform daily functions with an unrelenting sickness. In her analogy, people with a chronic illness or disability start the day with a finite amount of energy to spend on tasks the rest of us take for granted.

She illustrated this by presenting her friend with a handful of spoons — 12 to be exact. She asked her friend to describe the first tasks she would undertake daily, like showering and getting dressed.

If you've struggled with an illness or disability or know someone who does, you know that these two simple acts to start the day can take hours. It may feel like the biggest thing you accomplished, and yet you still have the rest of the day to go. Her friend lost a few spoons in completing these first tasks of the day. For every subsequent daily task her friend

49

described, Christine quietly removed more spoons from her friend's collection.

At the end of the exercise, her friend was shocked to see that she had almost no spoons left. Her imaginary day wasn't yet over, but she was almost out of spoons.

Christine was trying to help her friend understand the kinds of decisions she would have to make throughout the day about the smallest of things. Each seemingly simple decision would ensure she had enough energy to get the important things done. She also wanted her to understand how much tradeoff and planning Christine had to put in to every day to perform the basics of life.

It's a powerful analogy. You can find a link to the article on my resource page at **mymentalhealthmoment.com/bookreso urces**.

The Spoon Theory can be applied to stress and our daily lives

Even if you don't have a chronic illness or disability, you really only have so much energy and focus to dedicate to all the things in your life. And our modern life is making it harder for us to quantify where our best energy is going. So you need to make sure you're devoting your spoons to the things that will give you the best return on the things you value most.

Be intentional about who and what you give your energy to.

If you're giving someone your time, you're also giving them your energy. I don't think that's my introvert brain talking. I think that's how it is for most people. When you offer someone your time, you're giving away a commodity you can't replace. That 20 minutes you spent listening to your neighbor complain about the other neighbor is time you can never get back. This is serious business. Not everyone and everything deserves your energy equally.

I'm not saying don't talk to your neighbors or listen to the people in your life who need your help and input. But do consider the energy cost for everything that crosses your path and be willing to set boundaries, if necessary. This especially applies at work for those humans who cross your path to gossip. Gossip is a ginormous energy sucker and serves the purpose of also being negative. There are no winners in gossip world.

Ask yourself how many of your spoons you want to devote to others and their priorities today. Decide how you will allocate them.

Don't use all your spoons every day.

Pace yourself. Just because you started today with 12 spoons doesn't mean you have to use all 12 spoons today. It's okay to reserve one in case you need it tomorrow. Keep one spoon in tow so you can build some margin in your day.

I heard author and leadership expert John Maxwell say that as much as 20% of his day is spent in margin time. How is that possible? Do you know how many spoons John Maxwell must have thrown at him every day? (I'm now imagining him with his hands up defensively, deflecting incoming spoons.) He understands that his energy and time spent in non-productive activity and reflection is key to his success. It must work because in spite of his busy schedule, he has managed to write more than 50 books.

Margin is where insight happens because we're not so focused on making things or getting things done. This is a great way to reserve some of your energy and maybe have a little more for tomorrow.

Understand that you simply can't do everything.

I know you tell yourself this. I do, too. Every freakin' day. But on those days when you're completely frazzled, look back over your day. You'll see the places where you tried to hold on to every spoon at all costs. In fact, during the day, use your frazzled ness as a trigger to stop right where you are and start reflecting on your spoon situation. Are you focused on something that's not going to get you anywhere? Are you falling into the expectations of others instead of pursuing what's important to you? Where can you direct your best energy right now?

IN THIS MOMENT

- Identify those things in this day that are most important to you and will make the most difference in your day. Use your precious spoons to scoop up those things and let everything else fall where it may.
- Breathe yourself through "let everything else fall where it may."
- Go in your kitchen drawer and bring some spoons to work with you today. Place them on your desk and remove them as you spend your time. (Don't forget to bring them back home, though!)

DAY 12: How do you see your world?

One's destination is never a place, but a new way of seeing things.
— Henry Miller

What is the biggest thing that stresses you out? Is it your boss? Is it crazy traffic? Is it trying to keep up with your busy schedule? Or maybe it's constantly feeling like you're on the run. All of these external things play a big role in how empowered you feel in managing your day-to-day. But the way you think is the biggest predictor of how you well you will actually manage your stress.

When we're kids, we watch others around us and how they behave. We take mental notes on how to respond to things. If your mom freaked out on you every time you broke a dish, you may have learned that breaking things is a catastrophic failure. So guess what happens when you break a dish as an adult? You hear that voice in your head screaming at you, asking why you're so clumsy. But you may also freak out over non-dish-related activities — like being late to work — in the same way as if you broke a dish.

You learned from your mom that things that go wrong require a catastrophic response. That's an extreme example. Seriously, if you're still breaking dishes as an adult you may want to consider paper plates. But this illustrates how we get into unhealthy ways of thinking that aren't helpful to us.

You see the world through your very own set of lenses.

Your lenses were formed by the rules you made up about your experiences. Have you ever played a game with someone where they made up the rules as they went along? Were you frustrated by that? I certainly was. But this is kind of what we do with our life experiences. We form rules based on what we go through. For everything that happens to you, big or small, you subconsciously ask yourself a series of questions:

- What's happening right now?
- Have I seen this before?
- What should I make of this experience?
- What does it mean for me?
- What do I do now?

How you answer those questions creates your specific view of how you think the world works for you. So if the screaming mom was your experience, then everything you do you will want to treat as a very big deal. This can hold true for you even if the situation really doesn't call for it.

Everything that happens to you passes through those lenses.

Each new encounter adds another layer. So the next experience will have to get through this first filter in order for you to come up with a response. You tell yourself this is how the world works, and this is how I should respond.

But it's easy for those experiences to get distorted. In therapy we call these *cognitive distortions* (Burns, 1999). This happens when your lens is so thick that it distorts your view of what's really going on. You react based on how you've reacted before, not based on what's in front of you. And this absolutely impedes your vision and keeps you from finding solutions. It's also a big contributor to your stress.

A case of the "shoulds"

One example of a cognitive distortion is *should statements*. These are internal comments like:

- "I've been eating clean for a month now. I should have lost more weight."
- "I was so cranky at home last night. I should be a better mother."
- "I'm almost 50. I should be further along in my career."

Should statements set impossible standards for you. When you don't reach those standards you feel guilt, shame or anger. And when you direct those statements at others, you can portray yourself as the victim because others haven't met *your* standards. For example: "I can't believe my boss snapped at

55

me. She should know how that makes me feel. She's supposed to be a leader."

Should statements set you up for all kinds of emotional instability. They leave you feeling disappointed by yourself or others.

So what do you do if you recognize should statements in yourself? You may have to lower your expectations a bit. You may be envisioning some ideal situation for yourself that really isn't realistic for you. Or maybe it's not realistic for right now. And for other people? Well, you have to remember they're just as human as you are. As humans we will make mistakes, no question. We've got to learn to give ourselves and each other a little bit of a break.

IN THIS MOMENT

- Think about the ways you've responded to negative thoughts or events as a child. Do you see any patterns between then and now?
- Write down any distressing or negative thoughts running through your head.
- See if you find any should statements floating around in there.
- Make a list of more workable thoughts. For example, "I should be a better mother," becomes "I didn't handle myself the way I wanted with my kids but I will start fresh from here."

DAY 13: Don't make it personal

People understand me so poorly that they don't even understand
my complaint about them not understanding me.
— Soren Kierkegaard

As we introduced in Day 12, cognitive distortions are thinking errors that keep us feeling stressed and wrung out. They are patterns of thinking that can limit our view of what's really going on around us. *Personalization* is a great example of how cognitive distortions can impede our vision.

What is personalization?

When you think an event or someone's response is a personal reaction to you, you might struggle with this cognitive distortion. Are people always imploring you not to take things so personally? Then read on.

Say, for example, you and a friend make plans to go to the beach. At the last minute, she calls to tell you she has to cancel because her kid got the flu. Immediately you think she's just ditching you because it was so last minute. Her kid seemed fine yesterday at the bus stop. Now you're really mad at her. If you had stopped to consider other scenarios, though, you might have discovered a few alternate possibilities here.

- She doesn't want you to get sick so she's staying home to make sure you stay healthy. That's a good friend all day long.
- Her kid was fine yesterday but woke up this morning with a sore throat that became a full-fledged fever by lunch. That's how the flu works sometimes.
- She really wants to go but her mother isn't able to come over and be at the house while the kid sleeps it off, or....
- She's ditching you because you always take things so personally. Your first reaction is always a possibility but you don't have to go there first.

You're giving yourself the short end of the stick.

When you operate in this mindset, you automatically short-change yourself. Personalization places you at the center of everyone's world. If you're at the center of everyone's world, then you're responsible for their happiness or success. So you get to blame yourself when things that you don't even own go wrong. Are you sure you want to go there?

Take your micromanaging boss, for example. How many times have you complained about your boss' complete lack of trust in you? Obviously she doesn't think you can do the job or she wouldn't be over your shoulder literally all the time, right?

If you look at micromanaging more closely, though, you won't see a lack of trust or villainous thoughts about your skill set. What you'll see is fear and anxiety. And lots of it. Go inside your boss' head for a minute:

58

- What if this expensive project falls apart and they hold me responsible?
- I'm on the hook for this event to go well or I'm probably not working here anymore.
- No one is giving clear direction for me and my team, so I don't know what I don't know. What if I'm wrong?

With all that swimming around in her head, do you think it would be easy to not triple check everything your team is doing to make sure you guys pull it off? Her job may depend on it. Do any of these thoughts have anything to do with you personally? Is she even thinking about *you*? Nope. Like all of us, she's focused on herself.

Obviously micromanaging is not the answer to calm her anxiety. She needs to do her own internal work to manage her anxiety so her team can have autonomy and feel successful. But if you consider things from her perspective, you may see she's dealing with her own issues and concerns.

Personalization gets you so focused on how others' behaviors are affecting *you* that you fail to see how much *they* may be carrying. Personalization places you completely inside yourself and makes you feel like a victim who has to carry everyone's stuff.

Open yourself up to other possibilities.

Like all of these thinking errors, personalization puts you in a pretty extreme place. Take yourself out of the equation a bit and look for all the possibilities. People do things for all kinds of reasons that have nothing to do with you. Remembering that can help you give some grace to yourself and others, too.

IN THIS MOMENT

- Think back to a couple of times where you got yourself wound up by something you thought others did to you because you think they don't like you.
- Re-examine the situation and see if you can find any other explanations for their behavior.
- If they are currently in your life, decide how you might see things from their perspective today.
- Reflect on the outcome at the end of the day.

DAY 14: Put a label on it

*"You've got me feeling emotions, Deeper than I've ever dreamed of,
You've got me feeling emotions, Higher than the heavens above. I
feel good, I feel nice, I've never felt so satisfied, I'm in love, I'm
alive, Intoxicated, Flying high."*
— *Mariah Carey / Robert Manuel Clivilles / David Bryon Cole, from
the song "Emotions"*

When it comes to emotions, sometimes it's hard to know exactly
what you're dealing with. We don't always have the right words.
We start learning vocabulary words in kindergarten to describe
everything from trees to animals. But we don't get words to
describe how we feel. We can point at a dog and say "d-o-g."
But when we're upset, we're not encouraged to label it by saying
"m-a-d." So how should we know what to do with difficult
feelings if we can't describe them?

Feeling words help you build an emotional vocabulary.

Part of being able to manage your emotions is to be able to label
and identify what they are in the first place. Several adolescent
clients have told me that they get so frustrated when their

parents constantly beg them to tell them how they feel. How can they tell their parents how they feel, they say, when they can't even describe it themselves? Being able to speak from an emotional vocabulary is an important step in understanding what you feel so you know how to address it.

Usually, we group emotions into larger categories. In the later part of the 20th century psychologist Paul Ekman identified five basic emotions that he believed were experienced by all cultures around the world: anger, disgust, fear, happiness, sadness, and surprise. He and other scientists believed that these were the hardwired emotions that early humans needed for survival. These five emotions helped early humans know if they needed to defend a territory or respond to danger. Not a simpler time, necessarily, but maybe a little more clear about what constitutes danger.

Our lives seem more complicated now, and we live on a full spectrum of emotions that don't have the same survival implications.

- You may not feel angry but you might be annoyed.
- Maybe you're not disgusted, but you might feel suspicious.
- Maybe you're not necessarily happy but you do feel content.

Part of having good stress management skills is being able to identify and label exactly what emotions you're feeling so you know how best to respond. You can find a *List of Emotions* at **mymentalhealthmoment.com/bookresources.** Just like your teacher gave you a vocabulary list to study in the third grade, you can download this list and take some time to define each of these emotions.

How do they play out in your life? How do you typically

respond when you feel embarrassed, for example? What does it look like for you when you feel proud? Become familiar with each of them so that you will know when you're experiencing them.

Once you have a working emotional vocabulary, then you can use these words to quickly label how you feel in an emotional moment. You can actually make a verbal statement right in the middle of your emotional experience that describes how you feel. For example, if you're annoyed because you're stuck in traffic, you can simply state to yourself, "I am so annoyed right now."

This is called "affect labeling. "

Affect labeling slows down a part of your brain that's responsible for your emotional responses. That part of your brain is called the amygdala, which is part of your limbic system. It helps you manage your mood. Functional MRIs have shown this area of the brain quite literally cools down after simply putting feelings into words. Affect labeling produces a physiological response that dampens your emotional state.

That almost sounds too simple, right? Making a simple statement about the emotions you feel causes your physical body to respond. It may not make the traffic any better, but it will take the edge off the annoyance you feel in that moment.

But in order to label that emotion, you have to know what you're dealing with. That's why the vocabulary is so important. This is a great little skill to learn to help you feel less overwhelmed by the full range of emotions you might feel in a day.

Learning to identify your emotions is the first step to understanding what you're feeling. Articulating to yourself what you're feeling helps you develop helpful solutions. And all of this forms a terrific foundation for better communication skills with others because now you can explain what you're really feeling.

IN THIS MOMENT

- Visit **mymentalhealthmoment.com/bookresources** to download the *List of Emotions*.
- Identify some of the emotions on the list that you are feeling now or have felt already today.
- Make a statement about that feeling.
- Check in with yourself on how you're feeling after the statement.
- Practice this with someone else in the room. You never know, they just might validate your feeling!

DAY 15: Get what you want without feeling entitled

"You have to do your own growing no matter how tall your grandfather was."
— *Abraham Lincoln*

Have you ever thought about whether or not you're entitled? When we hear that word, we picture someone who asks for more than they deserve, or who thinks they should be able to cut to the front of the line, so to speak.

"That doesn't sound like me. I'm totally okay standing in line like everybody else."

Maybe. But entitlement can sneak into your life in some crafty ways. From my own experience, I can tell you that when I think I'm carrying too much, that's when I feel entitled. I've always been a hard worker. I meet my deadlines. I try to stay positive for myself and others. People know me as the person who can help you get something done. I bring value. I know that. But sometimes that backs up on me because after all that, when I don't get what I want, I'm taken off guard.

"In what universe do I not deserve to get what I want? Don't you see how hard I work?" It sounds pretty much like that. I may not say it out loud but this is definitely what I'm muttering under my breath. That sense of entitlement can eat away at my resilience to stress. How?

Resilience is about focusing on your strengths and accessing resources and options even in the face of challenges. This is where you find the energy to move forward to help yourself.

What about me?

Entitlement keeps you focused on what everyone else is *not* doing for you. Instead of keeping your eye on what *you* can do to get what you want, you start looking around for all the ways that people aren't helping you. So you start using language like, "I deserve more than this." There's always this tension between what you don't have and what you feel like you're owed. This is both an energy drain and a zap on your resilience. If you're wallowing in those kinds of negative thoughts, you're definitely not going to get what you feel like you deserve. And you're not focused on taking any action to go get it. You're stuck in a victim mentality. There's nothing resilient about a victim mentality.

Now, I'm not saying you shouldn't strive to be more and do more. You deserve to have the best shot at achieving your goals and dreams. Every human does. I'm talking about that constant undercurrent that says you should have more just because you're good and you've been around here a while. You can see this in your family relationships. Maybe you're the one who's always taking care of things and making sure everybody has what they need. They may not always return the effort. Or maybe they don't even acknowledge it, at least not when you want them to.

It's easy to feel like you deserve better treatment than that. And maybe you do. But by focusing on what others are *not* doing

66

to recognize your contributions, you can quickly lose sight of where you were headed in the first place.

Enter negative thoughts and stress.

All that negativity and rumination about what you're not getting can make your mood go south. Does the company you work for really owe you anything more than paying you for the job that you do for them? I don't mean to sound cynical. But at the end of the day, your company isn't paying you for all the extra gifts and "that special something" that you bring to your work. If you perform the basic job description you agreed to when you started, then that's what they're compensating you for. You're not really *entitled* to more.

So when you're doing all this extra stuff and you're not getting recognized, it's easy to feel like you're not getting what you deserve. That can leave you feeling less engaged in your work. Instead of looking to the future — where all the goodies are — you're stuck where you are right now. It can start to sour you on your relationship with your company really fast.

If you don't feel like you're getting what you deserve, you have three options to stay out of "Entitlement Land" and keep you focused on what's ahead.

One, you can simply ask for what you want.

Shocking, I know. But most of us don't do this. We prefer our passive-aggressive style of wringing our hands about what others aren't doing for us. So ask them to do something for you. This forces you to define what you really want and put words on it to articulate it. That in itself is a great exercise.

Second, find out what you need to do to get what you want.

You know as well as I do that if you really get what you want and what you deserve, it's because you committed yourself to take action. Honestly, there are few situations where other people truly have all the power to keep you from getting what you want. How many more levers can you pull to see this through? I know, you're already carrying so much of the weight. But to get what you want, you may have to carry a little more and forget about what everybody else is doing or not doing.

Lastly, if you're not getting what you want, maybe it's time to go somewhere else.

Opportunity exists in so many places anymore. You should always be assessing what's working and what's not. Sometimes getting what you want lies in another place. That's okay. It doesn't mean that you failed. It may mean that you don't have the resources you need in this place to get what you want.

Sometimes you have to look at what you have available to you and be brave enough to make the decision that where you are now just may not be cutting it. That really has nothing to do with anyone else. It has everything to do with you.

Feeling entitled takes away your power.

It's hard to get what you want, and it's hard to help other people succeed when you feel like you have no power over your situation. When you feel powerless, it's easy to slip into that victim mindset. That won't get you far. Explore a few tools to help you get in the habit of accessing what you already have.

Focus on what you can do now to get what you want.

IN THIS MOMENT

- Think of one thing that's not going your way, at work or at home. How can you ask for one thing you need or want in this situation?
- Take a minute to explore the possibilities if you simply changed your situation. You don't have to actually do it. Allow your mind to wander for a minute. How would your circumstances change if you explored other opportunities?
- Write those opportunities down and look at them. What steps can you take now to inch yourself toward those new possibilities?
- Visit **mymentalhealthmoment.com/bookresources** to read my series on resilience and stress.

DAY 16: Stop predicting the end of the world

We may be up against a stone wall, but we don't have to bloody our heads against it unless we choose to.
— *William Glasser*

As we've covered already, cognitive distortions keep you at extremes. Catastrophizing is one of the more dastardly cognitive distortions. This thinking style makes you the very worst predictor of disaster because *everything* is a disaster. When something challenging enters your life, catastrophizing will tell you that the worst-case scenario is the only possible scenario.

Having a tough time finishing your big project? Catastrophizing will tell you that you will never finish, and you'll look bad in front of your peers, too. Are you having a hard time sleeping? "I'll never fall asleep. And I won't be able to function at all tomorrow."

Thoughts like this leave you completely paralyzed for action. If devastation is just on the horizon, why even bother to try? So it's pointless for you to even challenge what's going on because all your efforts lead to one devastating place that shuts everything down.

Catastrophizing is one of the more destructive cognitive

distortions because it keeps you completely locked out of options. By placing complete destruction as your only outcome, you take yourself off the hook for any responsibility in finding more workable options that will actually help you.

Big changes can bring about the seduction of the apocalypse.

Change is a fact of life, and it happens in all domains. If you don't check yourself on this thinking style, the consistent changes in life will have you always looking for the next dooms-day scenario. One place you can always find catastrophizing is during organizational change at work.

Change at work is about as stressful as it gets. When a company restructures or pursues a new direction, it can feel like the floor is literally moving under you all the time. You almost never know what's really going on. You don't know what — or who — to grab onto for support. So there's legitimate fear. The knee-jerk response for many people in this situation is predicting doom. You'll hear comments like:

- "They probably want to get rid of us anyway."
- "Everything's going to change now."
- "There goes my pension."
- "I'll never be able to retire."
- "They'll probably bring in a bunch of younger employees, and we'll be out."
- "Nobody really cares about us. They'll overload us until we quit so they don't have to pay unemployment."

Yikes. But you know I'm not making this up. Every single one of these statements ends up with you, the employee, having no choices amidst all this change. You're the one standing among the rubble with just your red stapler left to keep you company. Queue up the victim mentality.

(Catch the movie *Office Space* if you want to understand that red stapler reference. Also, it's a pretty great movie about how work is.)

Back off the end-of-the-world scenario.

If you can think about this a different way, you can find some options for yourself. Often change at work brings enormous opportunities — but not if you're predicting the apocalypse in your head right before your next staff meeting. Catastrophizing is the easiest cognitive distortion to challenge because almost anything you challenge it with will seem plausible. After all, anything is better than destruction.

Think you'll never get to sleep? Science says you will. It's a natural function built in to your body. At some point you absolutely will sleep. Maybe not when it's convenient for you, but it will happen. You won't be able to function at all tomorrow if you're tired? Unless you slip into a coma, that's not a true statement. Granted, you probably won't be at your best, but you'll be able to do some stuff. So the less catastrophic statement here is:

> *"I'm having some trouble getting to sleep right now, but my body will sleep when it's ready. I may not be at 100% of my performance level tomorrow but I'll have what I need to get through the day."*

That's miles away from the drama-inducing "I'll never sleep again."

At work, when you're tempted to frame your job as an Avengers-movie parody, consider some other options that give you a bit of power among all this change. So, for example, the statement, "Everything's going to change now," becomes:

> *"Some things will definitely change but not everything. Maybe I can uncover some new opportunities in all this that will help me stand out."*

On the surface all this may sound a little like denial.

But I think you have to ask yourself, do you really want to walk around feeling like you're carrying the weight of the end of the world? Or do you want to feel some hope that you still have the ability to influence the things that happen to you?

IN THIS MOMENT

- Go over some of the more distressing parts of your day. What thoughts went through your mind? Were they about disaster and no-way-out scenarios?
- Write down some alternate outcomes for those thoughts that don't involve you having to shoulder the worst possible endings.
- Ask a trusted friend ways they've noticed you respond to challenges. What can you pick up from their observations?

DAY 17: Do good to feel good

If you want to have a life that is worth living, a life that expresses your deepest feelings and emotions and cares and dreams, you have to fight for it.
— Alice Walker

Having good mental health is all about feeling good, right? If things are going well, we feel happy and grateful that things are going our way. We may not actively seek out help or support because we have good feelings about where we are.

But it also feels good when you get things done, when you perform actions that make things happen for yourself. Sometimes you make those things happen in spite of feeling cranky or when life isn't cutting you any breaks at all. You demonstrate healthy behaviors regardless of how you feel. You wouldn't necessarily say you feel good but you can see that the train is inching forward. So that's good.

So which is it? Feeling good? Or demonstrating the behaviors that create good?

Welcome to our modern quandary.

I'm not sure we know which one brings us what we want from life. We like to feel like we're accomplishing something here but we also want to wake up with happy and content feelings, just because.

Fair enough.

Even the psychological community doesn't settle it. Consider the diagnostic bible called The American Psychiatric Association's (2013) Diagnostic and Statistical Manual of Mental Disorders (5th ed.; DSM-5). The diagnosis of a mental disorder is based quite a bit on observable criteria that look a lot like behaviors, because they are.

For example, if you're demonstrating symptoms of depression, you may:

- sleep less or more,
- isolate from others,
- lose interest in things you used to enjoy,
- become more tearful or irritable,
- lose or gain weight,
- become more forgetful,
- or abuse substances.

Those are all things I can see without asking you. There are also some subjective criteria for depression: feeling sad, hopeless or restless, feelings of worthlessness or thoughts of death. Those I have to ask you about because I may not be able to observe them. But the overwhelming focus in a diagnosis is on what behaviors I can observe about you. When those behaviors keep you from functioning well in your life in some way, that's usually when you know you need some help.

- You call in sick to work frequently because you just can't get out of bed.
- Your productivity at work suffers because you can't focus.
- You abuse drugs or alcohol. I don't need to tell you how damaging that can be in all the important domains of your life.

I'm not saying your feelings don't matter. But your *behaviors* are what can make your life so hard to manage. And that can make you *feel* unhappy or sad. It creates a devastating loop. So getting some progress going with your behaviors can go a long way to helping you feel better, even if for a little bit.

The reality is that good mental health lies somewhere between *feeling good* and *functioning well*. Most of us understand that life has ups and downs that affect how we feel and how we act. But one thing I've observed is how powerful behaviors can be on those days when you can't seem to put it together otherwise. Focusing on your actions can be an agnostic way to lean in to something more objective until your feelings decide to come along on the ride. So how can you leverage some healthy behaviors and actions to help you on the feeling side?

Make healthy behaviors a ritual part of your day, not just a habit.

These behaviors can be things like exercise, reading uplifting materials, or helping others. But honestly, a healthy behavior can be anything you can do every day that helps you. But here's the dealio: it has to become so ingrained in your day that you don't feel right without it. You need to make healthy behaviors a *ritual.*

Rituals are dynamic ways to change your life. Something powerful happens when you simply decide to allow space in every day for something, no matter what. A ritual means you commit to the time and you take action because you already decided you would, not because it's a convenient time. You know you have a ritual in place when others expect you to take that same healthy action every day. For example, your spouse doesn't make dinner plans at a certain time because he knows for sure that's your hot yoga time.

Keep in mind, it takes time to develop this kind of muscle memory with a healthy behavior. But once you do, you find yourself thinking a little less about the merits of the activity itself, and it's easier not to talk yourself out of it. You're on "go" mode, so you go. This will carry you on the days when you're not feeling it.

Find healthy accountability and real connection in your life.

If I can observe your behaviors — healthy or not — others can, too. You don't need to be a therapist to notice that someone is struggling, withdrawn and isolated. You need people in your life who will miss you when you're not around, notice things about you and who will check in with you.

Connection is one action that can improve your life exponentially. Loneliness is a feeling that much of the world is struggling with right now, in epidemic proportions. That feeling can be lessened by taking more intentional action in how much you interact with others. If you don't have connection in your life, it may mean you have to reach out to others first to get this accountability going. You get as much as you give on this one.

Know your triggers.

You know when you're likely to feel vulnerable. Have some go-to healthy behaviors in your pocket to counter your difficult feelings. On the days we struggle, one of the hardest things to do is to sit with those difficult feelings without knowing what to do. That's when rumination and obsessive thinking take over.

If you always struggle with a certain feeling in a certain situation, have a plan for what you will do when you have that feeling. If your coffee time this morning had you worrying about how the rest of this week is going to go, take a few minutes now to go for a walk. Exercise is a slam dunk for anxiety. If that walk works, make that your plan for when you feel anxious at coffee time. Then, any time you feel anxious in the future, you know you go for a walk. That's just what you do.

You won't have to think about it in the moment when your feelings have already hit the floor.

You need feelings and behaviors to feel good.

Feelings and behaviors go hand-in-hand for a life that helps you feel productive and purposeful. You need both. It's nice to feel good but it's not the only metric of a life that's taking you where you want to go. Part of good mental health is being resilient to handle the challenges that come your way and taking real action to stay on track. Leverage both your feelings and healthy behaviors to feel good.

IN THIS MOMENT

- Pick one healthy behavior that you can easily add to this day. Don't try to crush, grind or hustle anything. Pick a thing that you know will be super easy to start doing today. Please also pick something you might like.
- Look at the rest of your day and figure out the best time for you to perform that one healthy behavior. Make it an appointment on your calendar and set a whole slew of reminders to blow up your phone so you don't forget.
- Tell others about your time for the healthy behavior so they can support you, and so they won't keep you from the behavior with their own priorities. Make this time a sacred time that only severed limbs or household fires would keep you from. :-)

DAY 18: Are strong emotions bad for you?

"Negative emotions like loneliness, envy, and guilt have an important role to play in a happy life; they're big, flashing signs that something needs to change."
— Gretchen Rubin

How many times have you missed the mark with something because you couldn't handle your emotions? And then you chastised yourself for feeling such difficult emotion? How's that supposed to work?

You don't need a therapist to tell you that emotions are powerful. Emotions represent some of the most basic needs that we have as humans. The ability to love, fight for justice, feel joy, and move bravely through sadness is what makes us human. We are absolutely wired for emotion, even the messy ones that spill out from us on to everyone around us.

From the minute we enter the grand stage of our lives, one of our earliest, most basic needs is to attach to others. This happens through a profound process of love and physical nurturing from a caregiver. Attachment is a deal-breaker for every baby human to start healthy development. And that attachment process happens from powerful emotion going from one person to another.

The war between good and bad emotions

Since we're little kids, we are led to believe that some emotions are good, and some emotions are bad. The evidence for this is largely due to the behaviors that we demonstrate when we feel certain emotions.

- If I get angry and I throw something, then anger is bad.
- If I do something that pleases others and I didn't get upset about having to do it, then I must be happy.

One fun exercise I like to do with children is to give them a page full of different emojis. The faces range from happy to angry, and all points in between. I simply ask the child to cross out the bad faces and circle the good faces.

They waste no time crossing out the obvious angry face, the frustrated face, the sad face, the worried face, and sometimes the confused face. It takes them a lot longer to pick out the good faces. Once they get past the obvious smiling face, you can see the philosophical war going on in their head with silly face and rolling-eyes face. Those are fun faces, but does that mean they're good?

When they're done, I ask them to pick out one of the bad faces they crossed out. In almost every case they pick the angry face.

"What makes that face a bad face?" I ask.

"Because that face was mad and did something wrong, so they got in trouble for it," comes their reply.

I keep probing.

"Sooo...it's bad to feel angry?"

They look at me as if I suddenly grew a third eyeball right in the middle of my forehead.

"Yes, because when you get angry you get in trouble," they shoot back. "So you shouldn't feel angry."

And there it is. Before you even hit puberty, you're taught to avoid emotions that make you uncomfortable. Yelling back at your mom or throwing your Xbox controller on the ground is bad, so anger is bad. Unfortunately, well-meaning parents focus just on correcting the negative behaviors that stem from unhealthy emotions. Their focus could be better spent helping their kids listen to what those powerful feelings are trying to tell them.

Hearing what your emotions are trying to tell you helps you learn what to do to manage them when things get difficult.

Emotions are dashboard indicators that measure what's important to us.

They let us know that we should pay attention to something that's bothering us. Anger may tell you that you were actually hurt by a situation and you need to repair a relationship in order to move forward. You don't need to run from that. Contentment and joy may tell you that your focus on prioritizing your family is actually making you happier. Keep doing what you're doing!

It helps to think of emotions as less good or bad and more healthy or unhealthy. Unhealthy emotions can surely lead to unhealthy behaviors, but that doesn't make *you* bad. Framing emotions in this way gives you more power to actually feel like you can have some mastery over them.

When you lose your cool with your kids, instead of beating yourself up for reacting in anger and thinking you're a bad parent, you can spend some time trying to understand what's really happening here.

- Are you overwhelmed with all of your other responsibilities?
- Have you set up clear boundaries with your kids so that they clearly understand the role they play in the family?

Figure out what's laying underneath that unhealthy emotion. Do you feel like you're going to lose it every day at work? Maybe you feel like you're swimming in a cesspool of frustration, powerlessness, jealousy and boredom. That's a recipe for disengagement for sure. But this isn't necessarily a bad thing. You can tap into each of these emotions and investigate the situations that got you here.

Are you jealous of that coworker who got promoted ahead of you? Maybe you're feeling hurt that you didn't get chosen, and you feel rejected. Fine. It's okay to feel that way. Now you know that promotion was important to you. What role can you play to make any changes that might set you up more positively for the future? What other options might you have?

Lose the idea of good or bad when it comes to emotions.

There are too many variations on our emotions to think that one set of emotions is good and the rest are bad. Learn to be curious about what your emotions are telling you.

Emotions add color and joy to our lives. They complement logic and reason because sometimes things are not always so black-and-white as our intellectual brains might try to tell us. Even difficult emotions add value because they are a testament to what we've been through. And if we're still standing, our emotions and our ability to use them can show us what we're capable of.

IN THIS MOMENT

- What is the strongest emotion you feel right now?
- How have you perceived this emotion in the past? As good or bad?
- How can you use this emotion to figure out what might need a closer look in your life? What might be hiding under this emotion?

DAY 19: Get unstuck and focus on what's ahead

"You have brains in your head. You have feet in your shoes. You can steer yourself, any direction you choose."
— *Dr. Seuss*

Do you ever have those days when you feel just a little stuck? The whole thing isn't going off the rails necessarily. You're getting *some* stuff done. But you've lost sight of where you really wanted to be for today. It's hard to know exactly where to start again so you can get back on track.

I feel like that sometimes. It can leave you overwhelmed and pretty frustrated, especially when your to-do list is a mile long and the end of the day is coming fast.

Here's a little formula I pull out of my stress toolbox when I need a little bit of redirection. And you know I'm going to tell you to write this down, right? Yes, I am!

Visit my resources page at **mymentalhealthmoment.com/bookresources** to find out why I'm so gung ho on writing things down.

First, what do I KNOW?

What skills and abilities do I have that I can use to get myself going?

Chances are you have a core set of skills that you engage without even thinking about them. Take a minute to inventory those skills and figure out which ones you can leverage to start taking action now.

What things have I done before in this situation that have worked well for me?

Even though you feel stuck, you do have a history of accomplishments, where things went well and you were successful. If you did it before, you can certainly do it again. Figure out what's worked before and see what you can replicate in this circumstance.

What are the things I may be a little afraid to do but would make the biggest difference for me in this moment?

Identify one or two things that carry a little risk for you or take you on tiptoes out of your comfort zone. Don't go crazy here. We're not jumping out of the airplane. We're just trying to taxi this thing down the runway. Find one or two actionable things that could inch you forward into action and get you moving.

Second, what do I HAVE?

What resources can I put my hands on that can help me get moving?

Look around you and identify what's available to you in this moment. How can you ask for help? What areas do you have carte blanche to start taking action? You probably have more to work with than you think.

Is there any low-hanging fruit that I can act on to build some motivation?

I'm a big fan of low-hanging fruit. You see, because it's right there at eye level, you don't have to work too hard to enjoy the great feeling of having harvested some fruit today. Look at you! You accomplished something and threw some things in your bushel basket without breaking a sweat. Now that you rocked the lower level, the higher echelon doesn't seem so out of reach. You might need a ladder now, but that's okay. Sometimes that's all you need to get going. You don't always have to start with the hard stuff.

What are all the options I can generate from these resources? What resources have I overlooked?

Now that you have at least a few things going, you might find opportunities right in front of you. After high-fiving yourself for getting this puppy moving, identify a couple of new areas that you could explore. Action begets action. You may have missed an opportunity before while you were mired in all your stuckness.

Which of my best strengths can I call on in this moment to get some results?

Identify your go-to superpowers, the strengths you naturally call on when you need to make sure something gets done. We all have at least one. If you're not sure, ask yourself what others are always asking you to do to help them. That might be a clue to your best strengths. Hunker down on those strengths to start seeing some movement.

Third, what can I DO?

What one thing can I do that will make a difference in my situation?

One lever can make all the difference, if you pull the right one at the right time. I'm not a pilot but I assume this is kind of how planes work. Identify something that will move you closer to your goal and get you on your path. One thing. If you need to make a plan for it, it's too big. Drill down to the simplest task that would bring the most results right now and do it.

Who can I reach out to that will hold me accountable to move on from this stuck place?

This can be tricky but it can impact your motivation and results. Identify people in your life who have an interest in seeing you do well, not because they get anything out of it, but because they want to invest in you. It's probably just one person, and it may not be a family member. On both accounts that's okay. Let this person know where you are and what you're trying to do.

Be vulnerable and humble as they gently hold you accountable and keep you from yourself.

What is one thing I can do today to better position myself emotionally, spiritually, and physically?

Check your gauges on all your self-care. Does this stuckness coincide with a period of time without exercise? Time to take a walk. Have you stopped finding time in your day for reflection? Maybe schedule some time later today away from the cacophony of your responsibilities so you can assess your priorities. Take an inventory in your emotional, spiritual and physical life and see where you might have pulled away recently. Add in one powerful practice that can help you start the process again.

You don't always need to create a whole new plan to get unstuck.

I know it's tempting to create some new master plan when things aren't moving for you. Don't put that pressure on yourself. You don't need to start over. You just need to start from where you are.

IN THIS MOMENT

- Take some time to answer the questions above. It will let you process where you are now and help you feel empowered on how to move forward.
- Remind yourself that stuckness can help you. It forces you to stop and make sure you're continuing on the path that's right for you instead of blindly walking forward. In our

crazy, busy world, that's a gift.

DAY 20: Churn up change to get things moving

"People are always blaming their circumstances for what they are, the people who get on in the world are the people who get up and look for the circumstances that they want and if they can't find them, make them."
— *George Bernard Shaw*

Is it just me or does everything about the world seem to be changing constantly? If you're maintaining any vital signs at all you may feel this, too. Adapting to change and flexing with the times seems like a requirement anymore. We tend to put change in a negative light, though, don't we?

- Relationships end badly.
- We lose our jobs or our company reorganizes.
- Middle age brings lifestyle changes for surprising new health issues.
- Aging eyes now require drugstore reading glasses. *sigh* This one literally changes how you look at everything.

But change also can be a wicked catalyst for growth if you know where to look.

Change creates movement and friction that uncovers new possibilities.

I live on Florida's Treasure Coast. This area on the east side of the state got its name from ships carrying gold and jewels in the Atlantic Ocean in the 1600s and 1700s. Back then, hurricanes barreled through the ocean and sank those ships. So a gazillion dollars of treasure now lays buried on the ocean floor. Much of it is unrecovered and undisturbed hundreds of years later.

During a hurricane, the force of the water hitting the beach eats away at the sand on the shore and out in the water. It's cleverly called *erosion.* Erosion is violent and destructive. It tears away at foundations, destroys delicate coral reefs, and it can close your favorite beach for an entire year. But it also moves stuff, like gold coins that have been buried for hundreds of years, for example. It's hilarious to watch treasure hunters trip over themselves to be the first one to hit those waters after a storm. Finding loot worth possibly millions in the newly-stirred-up environment motivates these modern-day mateys to keep looking for change.

Your change may come about in less-than-ideal and stormy circumstances. Yet it doesn't have to stop you from looking for what's been buried underneath you all this time.

There's no moving forward without something changing.

Churning up your own change is the secret to staying engaged in your life and work. This is the dirty little secret of progress. No one ever moved forward and made great progress without something else changing in dramatic fashion.

- Gutenberg's printing press wreaked havoc on the way information and knowledge traveled around the world (it really didn't travel at all before that). His first printed book was the Bible. I'm guessing having the Bible widely available in print probably changed a few things, too.
- The railroad plowed an ugly iron path across thousands of miles and completely overhauled the routines and industries of almost every town that held a railway station. If you've ever told someone how your life got "derailed" then you know the railroad also forever changed the English language.
- Henry Ford's creation of a super-efficient process to build cars irreparably changed the horse carriage industry that had been a mainstay in the Golden Age society of the late 19th century. (Karl Benz is credited with the actual invention of the first gas-powered automobile, in case you're playing along at home.)
- The creation of ebooks changed how people consume the very books Gutenberg had enabled and has now almost taken out an entire retail industry. Ebooks also opened up an efficient new way for authors to spread their ideas without having to go through the whole "I hope I get published someday" song and dance.

The changes you seek may not be as vast as these. But the reality is that in order to see effective change in your life, other things that you hold very dear and that play a monumental role in your life might have to move aside. You may have to find some steely resolve to weather the storm that comes in and moves all your stuff around. *Side note: as a seasoned South Florida storm rider, I can tell you that literally every storm passes. Just sayin'.*

Get comfortable being the instigator of change in your life.

Honestly, you don't need to wait for a storm to come in or a railroad to blow through your town to make change happen in your life. If your job is changing, are you upset about the uncertainty of this unexpected change? Or is it more about the fact that you haven't been continually looking at where your next opportunity may lie, no matter how your job is going?

Moving forward sometimes means making yourself uncomfortable on purpose to see what might float up to the surface. You won't find life-changing floaties in the calmer waters.

Stir it up. Move things around.

Don't be afraid to ask real questions about where you are. Look for areas that have been in deep homeostasis for a while. Are you taking that homeostasis for granted? What can you start to move around that might not be working for you?

Don't go crazy and change everything at one time. Let's not shoot for total erosion here. Change one small thing that's not working for you. Then look for the opportunities in the sands of discomfort you create.

IN THIS MOMENT

- Reflect on the areas of your life that are super comfortable but could tolerate some new energy.
- Ask yourself how you could try something new in one of these areas that could challenge you a bit.
- What one thing could you change today that would generate

some new ideas for you?

DAY 21: You might be passive aggressive...

"Although I express myself with some degree of pleasantry, the purport of my words is entirely serious."
— *Robert Louis Stevenson*

You've no doubt heard the comedy bit from comedian Jeff Foxworthy called, *You Might Be a Redneck*, where he lists all of the behaviors that might tell you how to know if you're a redneck. (That seems self-explanatory, yet I felt compelled to explain it anyway.)

I'm no comedian but I have a little list I like to call, *You Might be Passive Aggressive.*

What does it mean to be *passive aggressive?* Passive-aggressive behavior is when you communicate your anger or displeasure about something, but you do it indirectly. Instead of approaching someone you're upset with in a straightforward way — with the intent of resolving a conflict — you let your behaviors do all the talking. This leaves the other party trying to guess how you might feel based on what they're seeing from you, not what they actually hear from you.

We tend to associate passive-aggressive behavior with people we don't like or people that are difficult to get along with.

And it's true, for some people, being passive aggressive is a way of life. But lots of people demonstrate passive-aggressive behavior. And it's not because they're bad people. It's mostly because they like to avoid the conflict that arises from a direct and honest conversation. Conflict can make people uncomfortable. Many times, a passive-aggressive person simply lacks the assertiveness skills to ask directly and politely for what they want. Instead, it's easier to show you and hope you get her meaning.

Passive aggressiveness is like the world's worst game of charades, where the actions don't make any sense and feelings get hurt.

Actually, that sounds like most games of charades I've ever played. So you can see how this kind of behavior might go off the rails pretty quickly. Being passive aggressive is not an efficient way to communicate. It's indirect and doesn't bring the real issues to the surface. But it goes on in homes, schools and workplaces every day.

So here we go, without the witty, southern Jeff Foxworthy accent, I present to you my version of *You Might be Passive Aggressive.*

- If you've ever slammed kitchen cabinet doors while unloading the dishwasher you asked your son to unload this morning, you might be passive aggressive.
- If you consistently show up late for work and justify it because nobody really understands how hard you work anyway, you might be passive aggressive.
- If you talk about your coworker's shortcomings behind

their back, you might be passive aggressive. Also you might be a gossip, just sayin'. (Watch out for this one, it starts wars.)

- If you avoid eye contact and give your spouse the silent treatment after he went on an unplanned night out with his friends, you might be passive aggressive.
- If you've ever used the words, "Fine, whatever" in a discussion about something you're having trouble getting, you might be passive aggressive.
- If you've ever used sarcasm as a response to someone and your neck got hot and red, you might be passive aggressive.
- If you've ever deliberately ignored a text or email so that the other person will know just how mad you are, you might be passive aggressive.
- If you've ever said yes to something you really didn't want to do, then silently blamed the other person for making it difficult to say no, you might be passive aggressive.
- If you've ever put on your very best smile and nodded in agreement like an Elvis bobblehead, even though you really, really disagree with something, you may be passive aggressive.
- If your response to someone who has told you no is to make them feel guilty by recounting all the times you've helped them, you might be passive aggressive.
- If you've ever "disallowed" someone to use their blinker and move in front of you in busy traffic because earlier they pulled out in front of you unexpectedly, you may be passive aggressive.
- If you've ever been asked to do something at work you didn't want to do and you didn't give it your best effort because it's not really in your job description anyway, you

may be passive aggressive.

These are a few examples. But in each one of them, simply communicating from your own feelings and experiences would at least get a better ball rolling. In most of these cases above, you end up looking moody and difficult to get along with.

Granted, this kind of direct conversation can be uncomfortable because the other person probably will have something to say in response to you. There absolutely will be conflict. But learning to identify your own emotions and express them in a way that honors both people goes a long way to resolve the conflict. You miss all that when you play this passive-aggressive game of charades.

In the end, resolving conflict brings you closer together because now you've been through something that required each of you to grow.

What does this have to do with your stress, especially your stress at work?

Well, how unhappy are you when you don't feel like you're getting as much out of your work experience as you would like to? How do you feel when you see others realizing their potential and somehow figuring out how to keep the pieces together?

Are they any better than you? I would propose that they are not. They may have figured out how to ask for what they want without making others read the tea leaves. Not getting what you want — and not being able to ask for what you want — is a sure fire roadmap to stress and anxiety.

Learning assertiveness skills can help you vanquish passive-aggressiveness. Gaining the skills to communicate directly and honestly with others will change how you engage with the world. As an added bonus, it can keep you from feeling helpless and left out. You're expending energy every day. Make sure you use all the tools available to you to get what you need to feel engaged, focused and purposeful.

IN THIS MOMENT

- Do you recognize any of these passive-aggressive behaviors in yourself?
- Think of an area where you feel like you aren't being heard, or you're not getting what you want.
- Visit **mymentalhealthmoment.com/bookresources** to read my article, "Moving to the center of conflict" for some tips on assertiveness skills and conflict resolution.
- Write down some possible responses that you could use to approach someone directly with what you need or want.

DAY 22: Two ways thinking goes wrong

"If an architect makes a mistake, he grows ivy to cover it. If a doctor makes a mistake, he covers it with soil. If a cook makes a mistake, he covers it with some sauce and says it is a new recipe."
— *Paul Bocuse*

Back on Day 12, we talked about how our thinking shapes the way we see things. How we process what happens to us often determines how we respond. That's why learning to identify thinking errors is so important in managing stress.

One thinking error that kicks into high gear when you're stressed is *all-or-nothing thinking.* This thinking style keeps you at either end of two extremes. As we know, real life is often lived in the gray areas. But we like to make things appear black and white with all-or-nothing thinking.

You see this thinking style in trying to live a healthy lifestyle. How many times have you sworn you were going to work out five times this week? What happened when you bugged out of just the second workout? You felt defeated, right?

"If I can't even work out two times this week, then I guess I won't work out at all. So this week is gone. Man, I can't even work out for a week!"

Slow down there, turbo.

You gave yourself just two options. Only one of those options meant you were successful. There was no wiggle room for a different outcome that still allowed you to feel successful. Had you given yourself an option to allow for setbacks — or even a middle-of-the-road approach — you might have found it easier to chalk it up to being human when you don't hit the mark on day one. That would have made you more likely to start up again tomorrow with the third workout, as if nothing happened.

"Go big or go home" isn't always a great strategy.

It sells lots of books and seminars, but it's a limiting perspective. Go big or go home only gives you two options. And one of those options can feel pretty devastating. We like to avoid devastating, if at all possible. There's little grace for mistakes with all-or-nothing thinking and a fair amount of shame. Who has time for that? Most of your best solutions lie in having a few different options to choose from.

Apply this to the things in your life that really challenge you. Where are you giving yourself only one option for success? Does being passed over for that promotion mean you're not successful at your job? There are so many factors that go into being a success at what you do. Advancing is one sign of success but it's certainly not the only one.

Are you stressing about putting the perfect holiday dinner together with all your family's traditional foods? Is there any room for taking credit for getting everyone at the same table together, regardless of what you're eating?

You can't reason with emotions

Another thinking style that trips you up is *emotional reasoning.* This is where you use all the overwhelming emotions you feel to decide how things are or should be. Never mind any actual evidence to the contrary. If you've ever seen a Hallmark movie, you know what I'm talking about:

> *Unhappy hometown girl returns home, sees high school boyfriend, feels a flutter in her soul when she runs into him at the hardware store, reminisces about what they had together, follows her heart and gives up her successful law practice in Manhattan to return home and help her true love run the hardware store.*

What? We know it's campy but honestly we sometimes do the same thing in our own lives, minus the hardware store scenario. When we're overwhelmed and stressed, all we know is what we feel or used to feel. That's how we know we're stressed.

Our emotions put themselves front and center. Instead of pulling back a bit to logically study everything going on around us, we draw on what we feel to form conclusions about things.

We make our feelings into facts.

We ignore any other possible explanations. So we say things like, "I feel ignored and disrespected at work. I must not be a valued employee."

Or, "I'm so nervous about attending that new group at my church. I'm such a weirdo."

We let our emotions take us to the very place we don't want to be. Emotional reasoning can easily become a self-fulfilling prophecy because we start to behave in ways that support the very outcomes we don't want. Now we feel even more overwhelmed because we're still not getting what we want.

This is why it's so important to develop a habit of capturing your thoughts in some way. When you write this stuff out, it starts to look ridiculous. But you can't see that when it's bouncing around in your head.

Don't be afraid to run interference on your emotions. They have their role in your playbook, but sometimes they have to let the other players have their moment.

IN THIS MOMENT

- Take inventory of all-or-nothing thinking in the areas of your life where you feel like you're missing the mark. See where you can find some grace for yourself.
- Think about a recent time where you let your emotions drive your decisions. Where did you let those feelings become facts in the situation? How did the situation turn out?

DAY 23: A nature prescription for stress

"We can never have enough of nature. We must be refreshed by the sight of inexhaustible vigor, vast and titanic features, the sea-coast with its wrecks, the wilderness with its living and its decaying trees, the thunder-cloud, and the rain which lasts three weeks and produces freshets. We need to witness our own limits transgressed, and some life pasturing freely where we never wander."
— Henry David Thoreau

Have you ever thought how odd it is that we spend so much time indoors? We are creatures that were designed to cultivate our own vegetables and fruits, raise animals for food and connect with the earth on a daily basis. You know, connect with the dirt part of the earth. That's how it's been for most of human life until the past 100 years or so. Then when we got fancy with our electricity, running water, and memory-foam mattresses.

So here we are in the 21st century scurrying from air-conditioned place to air-conditioned place. We gaze out the windows of our offices (if you're lucky enough to have a window) and comment wistfully how beautiful it is outside.

Some of us can't remember the last time we even spent any real time in any kind of nature. But science is showing how much we need nature to feel good. And it's not just about getting outside to get a little vitamin D.

Access to nature is a key part of managing stress.

A recent study showed that 20 minutes of being in nature significantly reduced levels of cortisol. Cortisol, as you may know, is the hormone your body secretes when you're under stress. Some of that stress is good, like when you need to get up and get moving for the day. Cortisol helps get you going, so you can get the coffee going (yes!)

But when you live your life all amped up and anxious, your adrenal glands are working overtime to keep the cortisol going just to help you deal with everyday stuff. That's not good for your body so it's important to find ways to reduce levels of cortisol.

The cool thing is that once you come in from being outside for 20 minutes, you continue to see reductions in cortisol for a few hours. So the effect lasts long after you come home.

Change your idea of nature.

You don't have to live near a lush preserve or a beach to get the benefits of being in nature. Any place that gives you that sense of being in nature will do.

- Maybe it's a small park in the middle of your busy city.
- Or a botanical garden nearby.
- Or a spot near a pond that you love.

This why I'm always recommending a short walk outside at

lunchtime. You absolutely get the benefits of stress reduction from the walk itself. But you get bonus points for walking outside.

Nature reconnects you to the earth.

More studies are showing the benefits of what's called *earthing* or *grounding*. Our bodies have an electromagnetic field. Not surprisingly, so does the earth. Those two electromagnetic fields can complement each other. But you have to actually touch the earth to get this connection going. You can connect with the earth's energy and ground yourself by simply going barefoot.

Research shows grounding can promote a sense of well being, reduce inflammation, affect the immune system and even improve sleep. You may have noticed this if you've walked barefoot in the sand at the beach. Don't you feel completely relaxed and calm? That's your body being electrically grounded by the earth.

IN THIS MOMENT

- Where can you find green spaces in your area? Identify places nearby where you can have lunch or take a few deep breaths.
- Can you leave a change of walking clothes or a camping chair in your car for an impromptu visit to a beautiful place?
- Go outside and stand in the grass barefoot (as long as it's not covered in snow, of course).
- Find pockets of time this week to connect with nature in your own way in your own space.

DAY 24: Forecasting fear

"When a resolute young fellow steps up to the great bully, the world, and takes him boldly by the beard, he is often surprised to find it comes off in his hand, and that it was only tied on to scare away the timid adventurers."
— *Ralph Waldo Emerson*

Hurricane season is the time of year that we South Floridians "keep an eye on the tropics," as our fine meteorologists say. It becomes a constant refrain. The minute a puff of air pops off the coast of Africa, the weather folks start tracking its every movement.

- Where will it go?
- How bad will it get?
- Will it even survive the journey across two oceans?
- When should we get *both* eyes on the tropics?

The reality is that most of these little disturbances won't even turn into hurricanes. And most of those who do won't even hit land at all. They become what we call *fish storms.*

Granted, when a hurricane does hit, they can cause complete devastation. So the threat is very, very real. But when you've lived here for a while, you can start to tell the exact point when the fear of a big storm becomes a real threat you should pay attention to and prepare for.

Living in a storm zone is like playing a great, big game of chicken with anxiety. You worry about a threat that technically could happen, but hasn't happened yet, and possibly may not ever happen. But very well could. How's that supposed to work?

Doesn't that sound like your anxiety? Do you worry about all the possible things that could wreak devastation on your life? Tomorrow? Ten days from now? A year from now?

Everyone tells you to live in the present and to let go of your worry. That you're living so far ahead you can't enjoy what you have right now. But if you let go of that worry, how can you make sure you're prepared for a possible hit? How's *that* supposed to work?

I'll tell you what I tell new Florida residents who come from the landlocked areas of the world.

Worry isn't preparation.

Worry is not an action you can take that actually does anything. When you worry, you're not focused on taking specific steps that will protect the things closest to you. You just want to keep all bad things from happening. That's not a reasonable strategy.

But when you prepare for a threat, you consider what's most important and put your energies into real actions that answer to that actual threat. You wouldn't put your important documents in a waterproof box if the threat is from wildfire. To be effective, the preparation should be appropriate to the threat.

Worry is not an actionable strategy to help you prepare for

the things that can truly rock your world. Ask yourself how effective your worry is in being prepared for something that could actually happen.

Use a little *if/then* logic on yourself. *If* I worry about this right now, *then* exactly how does it set me up to handle this possible situation later?

Every storm is different.

As much as you prepare, you can't plan for every possible scenario. There are too many variables in a storm to even come close to that. Some storms have destructive winds that tear through homes and businesses and leave a mountain of rubble in their wake. Other storms have more rain than wind. These are called *wet storms* because they contain so much precipitation that the devastation comes more from flooding than wind.

So if you boarded up your windows for strong winds, but didn't consider that your home is in a low-lying area, you can still suffer from the event. Being prepared doesn't necessarily save you from what you don't know.

Your obsessive worry about your job, your family and your health — with the idea of being prepared — still won't shield you from possible devastation. Something completely unexpected can still happen, but you spent all that time worrying about that other thing. You could have used that energy more effectively.

Don't let others get you worked up about the storm.

My phone blows up every time the weather folks start losing their minds over a new storm. Well-meaning family and friends from other parts of the country have seen the news. They urge us to evacuate, even if there's no threat. Thanks to our 24/7 media cycle and social media, we can follow these storms down to every painstaking detail, most of it completely outside our expertise. At this point, the refrain of the weather people takes on a more technical melody.

"The millibars are going down. That's not a good sign. We're watching that very closely."

I'm not sure what I'm supposed to do with that information. Is there a dial somewhere where we can turn the millibars up? Can we just do that, weather person? Some people will paint every doomsday scenario for you, if you let them.

Be a gatekeeper for what you allow into your world.

There are some horrible things happening in our world, no question. It's a lot to take in sometimes. But worrying about all the things that could happen to you on your way to somewhere very normal simply serves to feed your anxiety. And you feed that worry by:

- Listening to all the gory details over and over
- Commiserating with others who are just as worried as you are and
- Obsessing over all the minute details of a situation so you can play them back in your mind and keep the cycle going.

111

Ask yourself this question: *If I take in all this information, then what is my role in this situation?* How can I use this information to improve the circumstances? In most cases, you don't even have a role. And that's the real takeaway during hurricane season or in daily anxiety. You have no role in any event that happens other than being prepared for what you know and being available to help others who haven't yet learned. That's all you're responsible for.

Playing this role requires you to focus on what you know today and to plan for what you can. The rest comes down to your faith and trust to use what you have to weather the storm.

IN THIS MOMENT

- Write down a list of your current worries. What solutions are those worries leading you toward?
- Are the things that cause you anxiety pointing you toward the preparations that will help you make better decisions? Or are they creating busy work on your to-do list to make you feel like you're handing things?
- Who and what are you listening to? Assess your influences and determine where you can trim those influences.

DAY 25: Stay flexible so you don't snap

"We must always change, renew, rejuvenate ourselves; otherwise we harden.
—*Johann Wolfgang von Goethe*

One of the attributes given to me in most places I've worked is that I'm flexible. Now, isn't that fun? Who doesn't want to be known as the flexible one on the team?

I'm not sure when I became known as the girl who can adapt and go with the flow, but I can tell you it has served me well. I've learned excellent skills through the years to help me process my anxiety about change and help me find its place in my life. Staying flexible and adapting to the situations around me has helped me weather professional changes and a fair amount of personal change.

You see, to be flexible you have to be willing to give a little in places where it feels really scary. Maybe even especially when it feels scary.

The physics of flexibility

If you know basic physics — and really, who doesn't — you know that what doesn't bend will break. My first experience with this was at work on the top floor of a tall skyscraper in downtown Tulsa, Okla. A bad spring thunderstorm had rolled in one afternoon with strong, howling winds.

While I was standing at the copier, I felt the building swaying back and forth. I'm sure it was only a couple of inches but it felt like 10 feet in both directions. One of my coworkers must've seen my sheer terror while clinging to both sides of the copier because she quickly let me know that was perfectly normal. The building had to move and sway a little so that it wouldn't snap with the force of the wind. It turns out this is a deliberate and calculated architectural feat. What keeps this sway under control in many skyscrapers is a kind of pendulum called a *tuned mass damper.*

This is a giant ball, usually made out of steel, that weighs hundreds of tons. It's suspended on pistons and springs inside the building. When the wind blows against the building, the damper moves the ball in the opposite direction to help balance the sway. The building essentially becomes a giant tuning fork, bending and flexing with the waves coming from all directions. And most importantly, the building is still standing once the winds have died down.

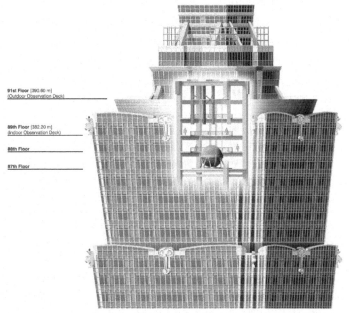

91st Floor [390.60 m]
(Outdoor Observation Deck)

89th Floor [382.20 m]
(Indoor Observation Deck)

88th Floor

87th Floor

The tuned mass damper in Taipei 101 Tower in Taipei, Taiwan -
Photo courtesy: *Someformofhuman - Own work, CC BY–SA 4.0,
https://commons.wikimedia.org/w/index.php?curid=3799263*

Be your own tuned mass damper

How can you bend and balance the sway of change in your life?

Ask yourself, Is this even about me?

In Day 13 we talked about the cognitive distortion called *person-alization.* This is where you make everything that happens to you a direct assault on you personally. One surefire way to stay inflexible and rigid is never to look outside your own perspective when things change. There's a good chance that this current change won't affect you, or it may affect you but have an even greater effect on others. Ask yourself, who else does this change affect most? What ways can I serve others during this change to help make it easier?

It's not easy to think about others when you feel that wave of anxiety and uncertainty. But it will take you out of your own head and give you something constructive to do while you don't know what's going on.

Go ahead and explore the worst possible outcome.

I call this playing the *What If* game. What's the one thing you're worried about the most with this wind blowing? Go ahead and walk that outcome out all the way to its bitter end.

- When *this* happens, then *this* thing happens, and so on, and so on.
- Go ahead and be dramatic with where the story ends up.
- When you get to the end of that story, ask yourself if that outcome is something you can live with. Not if you will *like it*, but can you *live with it?*

Most of the time you'll find you can live with it. You discover that you have the resilience to deal with things even if they're difficult. This kind of exploration takes some of the heat out of this moment because you find out in your little story that you probably have what it takes to withstand the winds.

Choose what you will engage.

To stay flexible you have to have the discipline to pick your battles. Not every difficult challenge is worth all of your energy, all of the time. Sometimes you have to find the humility to let some things go. Even better, let others discover what they can pick up and share with you. This is where you let the pendulum swing the other way so that you aren't bearing the weight of it all. You give up a little control here but you gain so much more in peace. And in times of change, how much do you really control anyway?

Learn to look outside yourself and make deliberate choices about what you choose to get worked up about. Be the pendulum you want to see in the world, I guess? Once you find what works for you, you may discover that you can take on whatever the wind brings you.

IN THIS MOMENT

- Review your list of anxieties and worry you created in Day 24. What are you making completely about you? Where can you focus on others?
- Play a simple *What If* game in your head right now with the thing that's bugging you the most. Let it play out in your mind like a movie. Watch how you handle that worst-case scenario. What solutions or workarounds do you come up with? You might surprise yourself.
- Write down a few ways you can put boundaries around some of your bigger challenges. Is there any part of the challenge that you can just decide isn't going to make the cut today?

DAY 26: How to calm the heck down

"I am never alone wherever I am. The air itself supplies me with a century of love. When I breathe in, I am breathing in the laughter, tears, victories, passions, thoughts, memories, existence, joys, moments, and the hues of the sunlight on many tones of skin; I am breathing in the same air that was exhaled by many before me. The air that bore them life. And so how can I ever say that I am alone?"
— C. JoyBell C.

Part of managing stress in our crazy, modern world is learning how to manage what stress does in our own bodies. What I hear from many clients is how out of control they feel when things start spinning. How do you make good decisions when you feel overwhelmed?

It's hard to come up with solutions and ideas when things are going wackadoodle around you. Maybe this sounds familiar:

- Driving to work this morning felt very much like running a qualifying lap at the Daytona Speedway.
- The kids won't stop..., you know, they just won't stop.
- Your boss completely changed how you do your work without asking how the changes might affect you.
- That creditor who calls every day has called you twice

already today.

You know you have to keep moving through the day. How do you gain back enough control to keep your head straight?

The best tool in your stress toolkit is deep breathing.

This isn't rocket surgery. I think we all instinctively know that taking a minute to breathe can give a little time to refocus. And we have to breathe anyway, right? So that seems easy enough.

But *deep breathing* is more than inhaling and exhaling with purpose. And it's not just breathing deeper, as crazy as that sounds. Deep breathing is a specific technique that allows you to use your breath to actually change how your body physically responds to stress. This is a powerful skill used by soldiers, law enforcement and other high-risk/high-pressure professionals.

With some practice, you can make deep breathing your "thing that always works." And here's the best kicker: deep breathing can buy you the control and time you need so you can respond to your stress in more helpful ways.

How does it work?

Deep breathing reverses "fight-or-flight."

The *fight-or-flight response* is supposed to be your body's way of helping you survive something, like running from a hungry tiger or getting out of the way of a moving car. Here are a few lovely things you can expect when you are in fight-or-flight mode:

- Your heart starts beating faster,

- Your blood pressure goes up,
- Your pupils dilate,
- Your muscles get shaky,
- Your stomach starts to cramp, and
- You suddenly start sweating.

If you've ever had a panic attack while sitting at your desk at work, these symptoms may also sound too familiar. There's no hungry predator at your back, but you feel completely overwhelmed, powerless and amped up all at the same time. Thanks, Body, this is a clever process to quickly remove me from danger. But I'm currently sitting at my desk not running from anything. I'm trying to finish my weekly report before I go to lunch, if that's okay.

Notice, too, that your breathing has gotten quicker and shallower. Instead of slow, deep, calming breaths, you're now taking quick little breaths from your chest.

Congratulations, you're stressed. You could use a deep breath.

Focus on deep breathing from your diaphragm.

The diaphragm is a nifty little muscular organ that sits right at the base of your chest. It inflates to help you pull air into your lungs, and then flattens when you exhale. The trick to deep breathing is to focus on filling your diaphragm — your belly — with air, instead of your chest.

Why is this important? Filling your belly with air stimulates your *vagus nerve*. That's a long nerve that runs from your brain stem down into your abdominal area. It's one of the most important nerves in your body because it regulates processes in just about all your major organs. Never heard of it?

The vagus nerve is kind of the introvert of the human body. You don't hear from it much until you need it. And when you do need it, it shows up with all kinds of practical solutions (high fives to awesome introverts everywhere). Who knew that expertise was sitting there all this time?

Well, your vagus nerve has been sitting there all this time — cleverly, right behind your diaphragm. The vagus nerve is responsible for ... wait for it ...

- Slowing your heart rate,
- Controlling sweating,
- Regulating blood pressure, and
- Keeping your digestive system relaxed and working well.

Taking intentional, deep breaths from your diaphragm presses on your vagus nerve, which sets about the task of slowing you the heck down. How about that?

There are some great tools out there to help you learn how to breathe from your diaphragm. Visit **mymentalhealthmoment.com/bookresources** for some apps and exercises that I use with myself and with my clients to build this important skill.

Deep breathing isn't a one-and-done approach

Learning how to breathe deeply gives you the power to instantly change how your body physically feels during a stressful moment. Making deep breathing a regular part of your day will help your nervous system stay conditioned to help you relax more quickly when you need it. But in order for it to work so powerfully for you, you have to make deep breathing a daily practice. Start learning the skill when you're already feeling relaxed.

Once you get it down, with some disciplined practice, you can pull this coping skill out on a dime when you really need it. You'll give yourself a better chance to respond to what's happening around you in those challenging moments.

IN THIS MOMENT

- Visit **mymentalhealthmoment.com/bookresources** for quick apps and exercises to learn the deep breathing technique.
- Try it out and take notice of the sensations in your body. Where do you feel relaxed? I know I'm finally calm when my gut feels relaxed. I know, that's weird, but that's where I tend to feel my tension and anxiety the most.
- Set a reminder for today on your phone that says "Breathe." Mine says "Breathe, already, would ya?" but I like to joust with myself a bit.
- Do that again tomorrow.

DAY 27: It is what it is

"Train yourself to let go of everything you fear to lose."
— Yoda

"It is what it is."

Have you ever said this? Boy I sure have! If something doesn't go my way, I take that deep breath and say, reluctantly. "Yep, it is what it is." It sounds like giving up, but there's a way to make "it is what it is" work for you.

It's called radical acceptance.

Radical acceptance means accepting your circumstances. Acceptance doesn't mean you approve of those circumstances or even expect them to change. But you help yourself understand that where you are now is where you are now. That's radical because that's really hard.

Sometimes it's hard to simply manage your emotions when things happen that you just don't understand. It's especially difficult when you're completely ruled by your past and your emotional response to your past. It's a difficult place to be and hard to change.

Radical acceptance can help you manage your emotional

self. You can't control what you can't control, right? You can't really move forward and take meaningful action until you acknowledge that things are the way they are, for whatever reason they are.

The serenity prayer is based on this idea. Having the courage to accept what you can't change is powerful. It allows you to leave a lot of junk behind you.

Radical acceptance is a deliberate and purposeful action.

It's like when you make a commitment to help your middle schooler with his science project. It seems like an okay decision at first because what's more common than a middle-school science project? At some point, though, the reality sets in that you may have no idea how to pull this off. Unless you became a scientist in real life, you probably don't remember much about science. And you haven't been in middle school since the 20th century. What do you know?

But you move past your fearful feelings because you love your child. You purposefully accept that maybe you don't have to know too much about science. It's more about the effort and the commitment to get the project done so your child can learn from that. And away go the two of you with poster boards, glitter and glue sticks in tow, ready for a grand middle-school adventure.

Radical acceptance means committing to accept something regardless of how you feel about it in that moment. It allows you to look ahead and weigh your options — the options you can actually impact. That's way better than looking back and wallowing in things that may never change.

Now that you accept what you can't control about your life, you can decide what you do have control over. And more importantly, what you can change.

How do you practice radical acceptance?

Stay in the present moment.

You can't accept things about your current situation if you're always living in the future. Stop and notice what's happening around you. Seriously, if you're at the supermarket, stop worrying about how you're going to pay your kid's tuition next month and check out your surroundings.

This is your life right now as it's happening. What do you see, hear, smell or taste? This will slow you down for a minute, and you might reflect on a few things you would otherwise miss. At the very least, it will interrupt your anxious mind with something else to do.

Stop running from your feelings and fears.

I know, I know, once you slow everything down, now you feel some stuff. Hard stuff that you don't like. Our modern world has conditioned us to run from pain and suffering. So we spend so much of our time fighting those scary feelings and thoughts. Wouldn't it be nice instead to quit pushing back so hard all the time? That's how anxiety wears you out. All that fighting against an unseen enemy eats up your best energy every day.

Take a deep breath (or 12) and let the feelings wash over you. It probably won't feel good, but it won't kill you. Now you're exposing your body and your mind to something that over time might start to feel normal, which means it affects you a little less every time.

Observe your thoughts and emotions.

So if you're not fighting your fears and you're letting all this uncomfortable sensation wash over you, what the heck do you do with it? Instead of fighting and interacting with all that anxiety, imagine yourself placing it on a leaf floating down a stream. I'm not making this up; there's a legit exercise called *Leaves on a Stream* that helps you do this. Visit **mymentalhealt hmoment.com/bookresources** for a link to the exercise.

Put some distance between you and your difficult thoughts and feelings. There's no law that says you have to let them move in to your head and start hogging the remote. Thank your brain for letting you know what's bothering you, then send those thoughts a wave emoji and watch those suckers float right on downstream.

Take action

If you can stomach the process to this point, brave one, you will find radical acceptance waiting for you. Once you've engaged your current moments and opened yourself up to them, you'll find the courage to see the wisdom in acceptance. You won't have to fight it because at this point it will really seem like the only option. That's how you learn to really mean, "It is what it is."

There's no magic formula for acceptance and no incantations that usher it into your mind in grandiose fashion. The whole process is a little anticlimactic, actually. The gift is in your understanding that you're not the sum total of your difficult thoughts and feelings and you can control how you respond to them. That's radical.

IN THIS MOMENT

- Read Day 26 again. Practice taking deep breaths from your diaphragm for five minutes.
- Visit **mymentalhealthmoment.com/bookresources** to access the *Leaves on a Stream* exercise.
- Try this exercise sometime today and record how your emotions and thoughts affected you.
- Write down a couple of areas where you are struggling to accept something you can't change. Practice this process on one of those areas for the next week.

DAY 28: Bring a vacation mindset to your weekend

"Every person needs to take one day away. A day in which one consciously separates the past from the future. Jobs, family, employers, and friends can exist one day without any one of us, and if our egos permit us to confess, they could exist eternally in our absence. Each person deserves a day away in which no problems are confronted, no solutions searched for. Each of us needs to withdraw from the cares which will not withdraw from us."
— *Maya Angelou*

If you're like me you have a long list of things you dream about when the weekend rolls around. Sleep is always on my list. I know you're not supposed to catch up on sleep on the weekend because it's not a good sleep habit. But I can't help myself. Sleeping in on Saturday feels like a little vacation day to me. I wake up when I'm ready. And I enjoy not one, but two, delicious cups of coffee brewed with love by my husband. I don't even have to make the coffee on Saturday! (yes!)

I get to enjoy reading without looking at the clock. I finally have time to fold and put away the clean towels sitting in the laundry room since last Monday. And I have time to do some odd and end things around the house.

It all seems a little sweeter on the weekend.

Apparently my weekend approach is a real thing. Researchers call this the *vacation mindset.* Recent research out of UCLA made an interesting discovery when studying vacation habits among working Americans. You've probably heard this before. Americans kind of suck at taking the vacation time they've already earned at their jobs. Some studies show that we take just half of our earned vacation days. Isn't that amazing?

Those same studies show that going on vacation boosts happiness and makes you more productive at work. (I'm not sure why you need a study to prove that, but there it is.)

In this UCLA study, the researchers found that some of the folks in the study treated the weekend as if it was a little vacation. It wasn't necessarily that they kicked back and didn't take care of chores or ignored their kids. They simply chose to focus on their present experiences and savored the moments in their weekend days.

We know how to savor things when we think we're allowed to. When you're on vacation, doesn't the food taste a little richer? Do you stop for a minute to think about how blessed you are while you watch your kids play Marco Polo in the pool? Do you enjoy impromptu long conversations with your spouse, without worrying about all the activities you still have to check off your list today?

For this group in the study, the weekend wasn't just another couple of days to focus on things you didn't get to during the week. It was a break from the usual, and it provided a respite from the intense focus and forward thinking we get caught up in during the week.

Big surprise. When the study was over, the control group

who used their weekends as little vacations reported higher happiness scores on Monday morning than those who treated it as the same old weekend. I don't know about you but I'm game to try anything that will make Monday seem brighter.

Here are a few ideas to help you develop a vacation mindset.

Do something physical outside

Take a walk, ride your bike, chase the dog, let the dog chase you. Let nature cleanse the palate of this past week while you do something good for your body.

Text a friend

Send a friend a smiley face, or a heart, or a fist bump, or that salsa lady dancing. Your friend probably had a long week, too.

Cook something simple and delicious

Lose your #keto, #paleo, #howmanypoints voice in your head for a minute and enjoy your food. Focus on good food that you made with your own hands.

Remove some physical clutter

Clean out the linen closet of those hotel shampoos you've been saving for eight years but never use. I always have a bunch of those. Donate them to a local homeless shelter.

Put some of the stuff you're not using on eBay, Craigslist, Offerup, Facebook, whatever

You get the benefits of less clutter along with some extra dough. Don't underestimate how much people love buying your old stuff. It's fun to watch others see value in things you've already gotten value from.

Write an outline for a book

Write about a skill people are always complimenting you on. Once you see the outline taking shape, next weekend you'll want to start actually writing the book. Who knows, if you write a bestseller, you might be able to take an actual vacation!

Give a lot of hugs

This includes side hugs, bro hugs or full-on embraces (be selective with this one, though). Hugs release a chemical in your body called *oxytocin* that gives you a feeling of well-being. That feeling is what we're shooting for here. You never know who might need a hug so you both win.

Use your weekend to recharge your focus and help you connect with what you love most about your life. Give yourself a little vacation this weekend!

IN THIS MOMENT

- Pick one of the activities above (or create your own) and schedule some time for it one day this weekend.
- Be present while you're performing the activity. Look

for opportunities to enjoy where you are in that moment. Journal about it so it forces you to process where you are right now.

· Set aside the urge to get things done for just one day.

DAY 29: Manage stress by living in the present

"I do not want to foresee the future. I am concerned with taking care of the present. God has given me no control over the moment following."
— *Mahatma Gandhi*

We live in the present, but we're not necessarily always present. This is where stress gets us. Our 21st century world is almost exclusively forward-focused. We're always thinking about what's to come.

- Create your own future!
- Prepare for retirement!
- Get ahead at work!
- Develop a life plan!
- Be happy!
- Change the world!

No pressure! We scoot around trying to take advantage of it all. We're so anxious to "get there." But once we get there, how do we appreciate who we are in that moment?

So many of our anxious and depressive thoughts stem from

this constant focus on some ambiguous future moment that will surely make us happy. Our future feels like it's always "out there" because it is. And even if you achieve all that you want, guess what? That future moment will — one day — become your present moment.

So how can you appreciate the present moment?

Getting a grasp on your present moments could be as simple as taking the time to focus on it. But you can be intentional about how to encounter the moments you're living right now in a way that helps you connect the dots. Here are a couple of things that might help.

First, create a done list.

You probably have a to-do list, for sure. But do you have a list of what you've already done? Don't look just at the checkmarks on your list or the things you drew a line through. Separate them and give them their own list. They deserve it! Those are the things you got done! The present moments that you engaged. Mark that!

Second, focus on how to master today.

Today is already here, and you're apparently already awake and moving around. Nice job! What are the things you can do today that will move you toward those future goals? Focus on those things, and shove the rest aside for now. Direct your energy and focus toward today's present moments and see where it goes. Don't let the future steps — which don't really matter right now — encroach on your present.

Third, stop moving.

This may sound simple, but in order to focus on the present, you may have to stop moving for a minute. Do you have to go right on to that next thing? Or can you take a minute to enjoy a little self-imposed buffer zone? Take a few moments to simply be still and drink in where you are. Marvel at how you're able to breathe without thinking about it.

I like to daydream in these moments. It gives my brain a break from all that analyzing and planning, which is my default mode. Let your mind wander for a bit. It's okay.

Stop moving when you feel like it's an inconvenient time and you can't spare the time. These are probably the very moments you need to connect with where you are right now.

Enjoying the present isn't hard but it does require intention. There will always, always be something in the future trying to call you out of it. Learn to engage the present on your terms to change how you feel about your future.

IN THIS MOMENT

- Stop what you're doing, put this book down (or put your device down) and gaze around you. What do you see that you didn't notice before?
- Close your eyes. What do you hear? Can you identify all the sounds happening around you?
- What thoughts are going through your mind right now? If you're carrying a particular worry about something, picture yourself placing it in a box and putting a lid on it. Shove

this little mental box into a corner for a bit.
- Take a few deep breaths (or 12) and enjoy the mental space you just created for yourself.

DAY 30: Be okay with scraping some paint off

"Don't be afraid to scrape the paint off and do it again. This is the way you learn, trial and error, over and over, repetition. It pays you great dividends, great, great dividends."
— Bob Ross

Before motivational speakers became an industry, there was a happy artist named Bob Ross. After a long career in the Air Force, he became a public television star in the 1980s and 1990s with a serene and mesmerizing how-to painting show called *The Joy of Painting*.

Each week we watched him paint a simple nature scene. At least that's what we thought he was doing. Bob was, in fact, dropping some serious wisdom on us while he moved his brushes and knives over that canvas. Quietly and patiently he would show us how to use the simple tools available to all of us — line, shadow and color — to create something beautiful. Something happy. Like a happy little tree or a cloud.

But he wasn't afraid to show the mistakes, too. The mistakes led to what he called "happy little accidents." These allowed him to find value in past efforts while creating a new direction.

Occasionally one of Bob's projects would require something

a bit more dramatic. Instead of starting over with a new canvas, Bob would use one of his palette knives to scrape off the original work. Scraping didn't remove the previous work entirely, but it did create a workable new starting point for the piece. By retaining some of what he had used before, he found a place to keep going.

I don't know anyone who enjoys scraping off the hard work they thought was going to be the real deal. But scraping can bridge you to the next part of the process if you can see past what's in front of you.

Have you ever been disappointed by a job that you realized just wasn't for you? What about a relationship you could see was going nowhere? Maybe this was supposed to be the year you decided to focus on your personal goals and instead you kept ending up right back where you started.

To scrape it all off and start over seems like a waste, right?

Am I supposed to be okay watching my past pile up in colored dust around my feet? What about my beautiful picture? Why can't I get what I see in my head to connect with the effort coming from my hands? Why do I keep seeing the same dull picture over and over? It's exhausting.

But there is some hope in all that scraping. The scraping is a necessary part of discovery. Scraping requires that you put your first idea aside, no matter how inspired you thought it was. That's an act of humility. You have to go through what's not working to find what does work.

So what if your job isn't what you thought? What matters is what you take with you from the experience that you can use somewhere else. Now you know.

Every experience matters and nothing is ever wasted.

All that scraping will be messy, yes. That's your hard work piled up on the floor around you. But that pile gives you the chance to prove that you have yet another idea up your sleeve. That carnage shows you that the learning process is fully at work in you. You're not afraid to engage it, even if it means your whole picture now has to change.

So leaving that toxic relationship lets you create the space in your life to learn what a healthy relationship looks like for you. You'll leave some good stuff behind for sure, but you won't need it because you'll be working on a much better picture.

Scraping gives you the space you need to get it right.

What did you miss the first time that you can add in now? Do you realize you need more "happy tree people" around you to support you in your goals? Go ahead and add them here. You have room for them now because you took away what wasn't working. You can put those trees anywhere you want now.

Scraping isn't a destructive act. It uses material from the past to create room for what's to come. It's the territory where the war between your past and your future is fought.

What will you scrape off and leave behind? How much will you leave on the canvas to create something a little different? Will you be brave enough to start scraping?

IN THIS MOMENT

- Think of one area of your life where you feel like you're always starting over or struggling to get traction.
- Make a list of lessons you've learned as you've walked through these experiences.
- What do you do differently now as a result of those experiences? How has this helped you?
- Visit **mymentalhealthmoment.com/bookresources** to check out an episode of *The Joy of Painting* where Bob Ross demonstrates what to do after you've finished scraping.

DAY 31: How do you want to finish?

"It is not your business to determine how good it is, nor how valuable it is, nor how it compares with other expressions. It is your business to keep it yours clearly and directly, to keep the channel open."
— *Martha Graham*

What are you racing towards exactly?

I read an article in *The Atlantic* magazine that set my mind asking this question. The article is called "How Life Became an Endless, Terrible Competition." I'll include a link to it on my resources page at **mymentalhealthmoment.com/bookresources** if you want to read it.

The author focuses on how work and life have turned into kind of a glorification of achievement and competition. For many, it's become a frenetic race of nonstop milestones and desperate grabs for status. And the prize for those who "win" this race is: more responsibility, longer hours and a constantly shifting sense of the wrong priorities. So the end of the race is not a place to arrive, to kick back and enjoy the spoils. It's more of the same — but a lot more. That doesn't sound like winning.

The author covers a lot of different territory in the article that's way outside my expertise. But his point here got my mind working.

Where is all this going?

For all of our daily efforts and the stress that we take on to meet our goals, sometimes we find ourselves asking, now WHAT'S the prize exactly?

Of course you want to advance, do well and make your mark in your career. You want to know that you're leaving a powerful legacy at home for those who are coming behind you. You're not afraid to dig in and do the things that will make those things happen. But you also want to find some meaning and purpose in each day apart from the constant focus on the next lap coming up.

> *Why are we okay staying so busy running a race we barely understand and that doesn't seem to really be getting us to a finish line?*

I guess we magically think things somehow will fall into place while we're busy taking care of stuff. I know I have to challenge myself with that one all the time. You can find destination and purpose and run your race well. But you may have to make a few intentional tweaks.

Let go of what's not working for you.

What are you currently doing that's not taking you where you want to go? Ask yourself what you're getting from that activity or that relationship. You may instinctively think you're getting nothing at all, especially if there's a lot of negativity involved.

But if you look closely, you may see that some of the things currently frustrating you the most are, in fact, meeting some kind of emotional need. And that's why it's so hard to let go of them.

I think this comes back to knowing your values. Where do you really want to go? Values are lifelong pursuits. There's no finish line with values because they're ongoing as long as you're breathing. This could be things like being a good parent, contributing in a positive way to society or helping others reach their goals.

It's really easy for your values to get overwhelmed by your more finite, urgent responsibilities. Sure, you want to be a good parent, but you also have to pay your mortgage. So that extra time at work on your kid's soccer tournament day can somehow take precedence. If every day feels like you're running up on the down escalator, look at your life and assess exactly where your values are being crowded out.

Make time for reflection and experience.

On those days when you go from thing, to thing, to thing, it's hard to find time to stop and look back over your day. Where were your wins? What did you miss? What can you give yourself credit for?

This is like watching films after a football game. Successful teams always go back and watch their performance. They look for improvement opportunities they couldn't see while they were in the middle of it all on the field. That's their time to make changes that will help them improve their performance in the next game.

Find a few minutes every day to schedule this "film time" for yourself.

- What should you be doing more of?
- What could you reassess?
- What can you just cut entirely?

Find that small nugget of time to put yourself through these paces. It might change your pace in the race.

Stay in your lane.

A visiting pastor to my church spoke about this, and it hit me squarely in the face. If you run a race with your head turned sideways, always looking around to see what others are up to, you'll lose for sure. The race is in front of you, for crying out loud, and it's *your* race. You can go as fast or as slow as you want.

Running this sideways race is distracting and dangerous. It's reactive and stressful because you're always responding to what's happening around you without considering what might be up ahead. That's a great way to run into something you don't expect. I mean, in any race, you're likely to run into things you don't expect. But not looking where you're going will increase those odds.

This doesn't mean that you shouldn't be aware of others who are struggling to run their own race. If you can lend a hand to a fellow runner, you absolutely should. If you're getting all wrapped up in their race, though, you may be keeping them from looking ahead, too. Now you're both running sideways. Where do you think that might end up?

When you know your values, you know where you want your

race to end up. How someone else runs their race won't get you where you want to go.

Life doesn't have to be an endless, terrible competition with no clear destination. You can run your race with vision, purpose and clarity. You can realize your goals and dreams and live your values right to the finish line.

IN THIS MOMENT

- Make a list of three key values in your life. These are "big picture" items that include how you want to grow as a person and what you want to see in your relationships.
- What problems or issues do you need to work on in order to grow in these values?
- How do the everyday responsibilities in your life point you toward these values?
- What do you need to change in order to stay in your lane?

Conclusion

"A peasant must sit in his chair with his mouth open for a very long time before a roast duck will fly in."
— Chinese Proverb

All of these *Mental Health Moments* are driven by something deeper than waiting passively to handle what comes at you each day. Our modern existence has conditioned us to reactively swat back at our lives and deflect the uncomfortable stuff. Our lack of stillness keeps us from spending time with ourselves in peace and silence. Our bodies are in constant motion and so, now, are our minds.

Part of handling your stress effectively is knowing what you want, opening up to the possibilities you have in front of you now and taking action.

In order to see any real change happen in your life, you have to hone in on the values discussed in Day 31. Values are the beacons we use to navigate our lives. We have to be proactive and assess how the rest of our lives are stacking up against those values. This kind of reflection won't happen on a whim. Our whack-a-mole lifestyles won't let it.

Living and growing in your values isn't just about choosing priorities.

We can easily choose priorities if we simply give ourselves enough time and space. Priorities are about making sure we're not only doing unimportant tasks, things that don't really lead anywhere. We can sit down and look at the activities that will give us the most return, maybe even putting them in a quadrant or matrix, if you roll like that.

But what happens when those priorities — in their worthiness — still don't seem to be leading anywhere? Maybe we haven't really examined our values.

Values are the driving force behind everything we do.

We don't often write them out or memorize them. When life presents difficult challenges, we don't stop and analyze how this particular situation fits in with our overall values. Many times it's easier to go with what's right in front of us because it's demanding the most attention. But having a good grasp of your values can actually make decision-making a whole lot easier.

Life today has evolved into a race to finish something that feels undefined.

- We complete stuff.
- We cross things off our list.
- We accomplish.
- We feel pretty good about all that.

But at the end of the day, sometimes we're not sure what all this is adding up to. So we feel like we're always struggling to get everything that's important to us swimming in the same lane as our values. And we're starting to get a little tired of all that moving around in the pool. That's when we start feeling helpless and stressed.

How do you define better values for yourself?

How can you create a vision for values that you can point to in a pivotal moment? Values that will light up your path like a summer carnival? It's really no different than breaking a project down into smaller chunks. But first, you have to define who you want to be.

Let's say you want to be a good parent. What does that look like? Close your eyes and imagine yourself being the parent you envisioned when you were waiting for this little creature to arrive. Are you available to run alongside them as they learn the simple basics? Are you patient in coaching them through challenges instead of just delivering a set of instructions? Can you practice the humility to truly hear what's in their heart as they navigate their own values, even if those values are a little different from yours?

Many good people value their ability to lead their community. Who doesn't want to have an impact in the face of so much that seems to be going wrong in our communities?

How can you better define your leadership value to keep it from feeling like another drain on your time and energy? Do you want those most vulnerable to better connect with their financial independence as a result of your leadership in this space? Are you focused on helping others develop a spiritual practice that will help them through their own difficult times?

Do you want younger generations to have a model for how to reach their own goals in a constantly-changing world?

These questions help you frame how you might function inside those values.

Where do you want to end up?

Determine one or two values that speak to your skills, experiences and desires. What does it look like when you are realizing that value in its full capacity? If you're successful in developing this value for yourself, what does it look like for you to be operating well in each of these areas? See what interesting and exciting things you can come up with.

There are no right or wrong answers because — other than math and some delicious bakery cookies in New York City — life isn't always black-and-white. You get to decide what you pay attention to, even if you've come to feel a bit trapped by ill-defined priorities.

Don't try to do too much.

Most of the negative stress we experience is because we are trying to do too much of what's not really taking us anywhere. That's where we feel the drain on our energy and life. When you put your focus on concrete values, values that are focused on specific skills and actions, you may find is that it's easier to decide what stays on your plate on any given morning. Having a better picture of where you're headed helps you make choices that get you closer to the kind of person you want to be.

Create your own Mental Health Moments

You won't have mastery over your stress until you examine your values. Take the time to decide what you want from your life and what you want to leave behind.

Take your values into your own moments in each day. Use those values to serve others. This is a great way to create your very own *Mental Health Moments.*

What can I do next?

Congratulations, you finished the whole book! According to a 2019 Pew Research study, 27% of adults in the United States didn't read a book at all in the past 12 months. So you are taking real steps to improve yourself in spite of everything whirling around you.

How can you keep the Mental Health Moment vibe going?

There are a few key things you can do to keep taking healthy actions to change your life. Here are a few suggestions:

Go back through the book.

Visit the pages you bookmarked or highlighted. Make sure you try some of the suggestions there. Don't pick a bunch. Just maybe one for this week. See how it goes and make any additional changes. Drop me an email lori@mymentalhealthm oment.com and let me know how you're doing.

Visit the book resources page.

In case you missed it somehow, visit the page at **mymentalh ealthmoment.com/bookresources**. This is a list of several resources I've referred to throughout the book. Feel free to bookmark it because I think of new things all the time. I'll keep adding to the page, even for stuff I didn't think of when I published the book. It's like a little bonus section for you.

Join my email list.

It's easy to join. Visit **mymentalhealthmoment.com/subscrib e.** I know you probably are on a ton of other lists and wonder about getting on yet another one.

Here's the thing: Social media has become so incredibly noisy, overbearing and distracting. I'm so over it. But email still feels like I'm talking directly to you so I'm going to focus more on email than just about anywhere else.

So if you want to get the latest on mental health, updates on what I'm working on for you, or you want to ask a question, you're going to want to get on my list. **No spam or ridiculous upsells to keep you buying stuff. Just me and you having some *Mental Health Moments.***

It would be so lovely...

One of my own values is to contribute to the lives of others in helpful ways. So, if this book has been helpful to you, then I'm pretty happy.

Chances are that if you have benefitted from this book, then others in your life might find it helpful, too. It would so lovely — and there would be significant icing on the cake for me — if you could share this book.

Here are a few ways to spread the Mental Health Moment message around your part of the world:

- **Text, email or message your friends** a link to **mymentalh ealthmoment.com** so they can check out the book for themselves.
- **Join my email list** at **mymentalhealthmoment.com/subs cribe** so you can get all my recent updates and the latest information in mental health. When you get those emails, you can easily forward them to people in your network. *(I'm not a spammer or upseller so I won't drown you in pitchy emails. I love sharing what might actually help you so you'll get useful stuff, I promise.)*
- **Let me know how the book helped you** by emailing me at lori@mymentalhealthmoment.com.
- **Leave me a review of this book** on Amazon, Goodreads, or

BookBub so you can share your feedback with others who are looking for a few *Mental Health Moments* in their day, too.

Notes

1. Ridaura, V., & Belkaid, Y. (2015). Gut microbiota: the link to your second brain. *Cell*, *161*(2), 193-194. Retrieved from: https://www.sciencedirect.com/science/article/pii/S009 2867415003530

2. Watling, J., Pawlik, B., Scott, K., Booth, S., & Short, M. A. (2017). Sleep loss and affective functioning: more than just mood. *Behavioral sleep medicine*, *15*(5), 394-409. Retrieved from: https://www.tandfonline.com/doi/abs/ 10.1080/15402002.2016.1141770

3. Jerath, R., Crawford, M. W., Barnes, V. A., & Harden, K. (2015). Self-regulation of breathing as a primary treatment for anxiety. *Applied psychophysiology and biofeedback*, *40*(2), 107-115. Retrieved from: https://link.springer.com /article/10.1007/s10484-015-9279-8

4. Neville, Morgan. (Producer), Capotosto, Caryn. (Producer), Ma, Nicholas. (Producer) & Neville, Morgan. (Director). (2018). *Won't You Be My Neighbor?* [Motion Picture]. USA: Tremolo Productions.

5. Grossman, P., Niemann, L., Schmidt, S., & Walach, H. (2004). Mindfulness-based stress reduction and health benefits: A meta-analysis. *Journal of psychosomatic research*, *57*(1), 35-43. Retrieved from: https://www.scienc edirect.com/science/article/pii/S0022399903005737

6. Gu, J., Strauss, C., Bond, R., & Cavanagh, K. (2015). How do mindfulness-based cognitive therapy and mindfulness-based stress reduction improve mental health and wellbeing? A systematic review and meta-analysis of mediation studies. *Clinical psychology review*, 37, 1-12. Retrieved from: https://www.sciencedirect.com/science/article/pii/S027 2735815000197

7. Björling, E. A., Stevens, C., & Singh, N. B. (2019). Participatory Pilot of an Art-Based Mindfulness Intervention for Adolescent Girls With Headache. *Art Therapy*, 1-7. Retrieved from: https://www.tandfonline.com/doi/abs/ 10.1080/07421656.2019.1609325?journalCode=uart20

8. Hülsheger, U. R., Alberts, H. J., Feinholdt, A., & Lang, J. W. (2013). Benefits of mindfulness at work: the role of mindfulness in emotion regulation, emotional exhaustion, and job satisfaction. *Journal of Applied Psychology*, 98(2), 310. Retrieved from: https://psycnet.apa.org/doiLanding ?doi=10.1037/a0031313.

9. Cavanagh, K., Strauss, C., Forder, L., & Jones, F. (2014). Can mindfulness and acceptance be learnt by self-help?: A systematic review and meta-analysis of mindfulness and acceptance-based self-help interventions. *Clinical psychology review*, 34(2), 118-129. Retrieved from: https://w ww.sciencedirect.com/science/article/pii/S02727358140 00026

10. Mills, J., Wand, T., & Fraser, J. A. (2018). Exploring the meaning and practice of self-care among palliative care nurses and doctors: a qualitative study. *BMC palliative care*, 17(1), 63. Retrieved from: https://bmcpalliatcare.biomed central.com/articles/10.1186/s12904-018-0318-0.

11. Miserandino, C. (2003). The spoon theory. *But You Don't*

Look Sick. Retrieved from: https://balanceanddizziness.org/pdf/TheSpoonTheory.pdf.

12. Epstein, N. (1980). Social consequences of assertion, aggression, passive aggression, and submission: Situational and dispositional determinants. *Behavior Therapy*, *11*(5), 662-669. Retrieved from: https://www.sciencedirect.com/science/article/abs/pii/S0005789480800050.

13. Lejuez, C. W., Hopko, D. R., & Hopko, S. D. (2001). A brief behavioral activation treatment for depression: Treatment manual. *Behavior Modification*, *25*(2), 255-286. Retrieved from: https://journals.sagepub.com/doi/abs/10.1177/0145445501252005.

14. John, O. P., & Gross, J. J. (2004). Healthy and unhealthy emotion regulation: Personality processes, individual differences, and life span development. *Journal of personality*, *72*(6), 1301-1334. Retrieved from: https://onlinelibrary.wiley.com/doi/abs/10.1111/j.1467-6494.2004.00298.x.

15. White, M.P., Alcock, I., Grellier, J. *et al.* Spending at least 120 minutes a week in nature is associated with good health and wellbeing. *Sci Rep* **9,** 7730 (2019) doi:10.1038/s41598-019-44097-3. Retrieved from: https://www.nature.com/articles/s41598-019-44097-3

16. Hunter, M. R., Gillespie, B. W., & Chen, S. Y. P. (2019). Urban nature experiences reduce stress in the context of daily life based on salivary biomarkers. *Frontiers in psychology*, *10*, 722. Retrieved from: https://www.frontiersin.org/articles/10.3389/fpsyg.2019.00722/full

17. Chevalier, G., Sinatra, S. T., Oschman, J. L., Sokal, K., & Sokal, P. (2012). Earthing: health implications of reconnecting the human body to the Earth's surface electrons.

Journal of environmental and public health, 2012, 291541. Retrieved from: https://www.ncbi.nlm.nih.gov/pmc/articles/PMC3265077/

18. Blumenthal, J. A., Smith, P. J., Mabe, S., Hinderliter, A., Lin, P.-H., Liao, L., ... Sherwood, A. (2018). Lifestyle and neurocognition in older adults with cognitive impairments. *Neurology*, 92(3). Retrieved from: https://n.neurology.org/content/92/3/e212.abstract

19. Erickson, K. I., Raji, C. A., Lopez, O. L., Becker, J. T., Rosano, C., Newman, A. B., ... & Kuller, L. H. (2010). Physical activity predicts gray matter volume in late adulthood: the Cardiovascular Health Study. *Neurology*, 75(16), 1415-1422. Retrieved from: https://n.neurology.org/content/75/16/1415.short

20. Meltzer, M. E. (2015). The Use of Acceptance to Promote Positive Change by Decreasing Shame and Guilt: A Practice Exemplar. *Issues in mental health nursing*, 36(10), 826-830. Retrieved from: https://www.tandfonline.com/doi/abs/10.3109/01612840.2015.1043673

21. Ekman, P. (1992). An argument for basic emotions. *Cognition & emotion*, 6(3-4), 169-200. Retrieved from: https://www.tandfonline.com/doi/abs/10.1080/02699939208411068

22. Lieberman, M. D., Eisenberger, N. I., Crockett, M. J., Tom, S. M., Pfeifer, J. H., & Way, B. M. (2007). Putting feelings into words. *Psychological science*, 18(5), 421-428. Retrieved from: https://www.ncbi.nlm.nih.gov/pubmed/17576282

23. Liu, S., Liu, Q., Tabuchi, M., & Wu, M. N. (2016). Sleep drive is encoded by neural plastic changes in a dedicated circuit. *Cell*, 165(6), 1347-1360. Retrieved from: https://www.sciencedirect.com/science/article/pii/S0092867416304044

24. Holt-Lunstad, J. (2017). The potential public health relevance of social isolation and loneliness: Prevalence, epidemiology, and risk factors. *Public Policy & Aging Report*, 27(4), 127-130. Retrieved from: https://academic.oup.com/ppar/article/27/4/127/4782506

25. The Gutenberg Bible. (n.d.). Retrieved from https://www.hrc.utexas.edu/gutenberg-bible/.

26. Sulzberger, C. (2004). An early road warrior: electric vehicles in the early years of the automobile. *IEEE Power and Energy Magazine*, 2(3), 66-71. Retrieved from: https://ieeexplore.ieee.org/abstract/document/1293606.

27. Connor, J. J. (2003). *Structural Motion Control* (pp. 217-285). Pearson Education, Inc. Retrieved from: https://engineering.purdue.edu/~ce573/Documents/Intro%20to%20Structural%20Motion%20Control_Chapter4.pdf

28. Fried, C. (2019). *Vacation Mindset: How Weekends Can Be More Refreshing.* [online] UCLA Anderson School of Management. Available at: https://www.anderson.ucla.edu/faculty-and-research/anderson-review/vacation-mindset.

29. Wilson, K. G., & Murrell, A. R. (2004). Values work in acceptance and commitment therapy. *Mindfulness and acceptance: Expanding the cognitive-behavioral tradition*, 120-151. Retrieved from: https://www.researchgate.net/profile/Kathleen_Palm_Reed/publication/232494484_Acceptance_Mindfulness_and_Trauma/links/00b7d51a7934787fb2000000.pdf#page=137.

30. Andrew, P. (2019). *Who doesn't read books in America?.* [online] Pew Research Center. Available at: https://www.pewresearch.org/fact-tank/2019/09/26/who-doesnt-read-books-in-america/.

31. Burns, D. D. (1999). *The feeling good handbook, Rev.* Plume/Penguin Books.
32. American Psychiatric Association. (2013). Diagnostic and statistical manual of mental disorders (5th ed.). https://doi.org/10.1176/appi.books.9780890425596

About the Author

Lori R. Miller is a licensed mental health counselor and emotional wellness consultant in South Florida. She owns a private practice, where she helps her clients effectively handle anxiety, fear, depression and other issues keeping them from the life they want. You can find all of Lori's latest books, articles and videos at **mymentalhealthmoment.com**.

In addition to writing, Lori shares her expertise on living a healthy life through online programs, seminars and consulting. You can contact her for speaking opportunities at lori@mymentalhealthmoment.com.

Don't forget to visit the FREE resources page for this book at: **http://mymentalhealthmoment.com/bookresources**

You can connect with me on:

🌐 http://www.mymentalhealthmoment.com

🔗 https://www.youtube.com/LoriMiller

🔗 https://www.bookbub.com/authors/lori-r-miller

🔗 https://www.goodreads.com/lorirmiller

Subscribe to my newsletter:

✉ http://www.mymentalhealthmoment.com/subscribe